# SUSAN DUCKWORTH'S KNITTING

# SUSAN DUCKWORTH'S KNITTING

BALLANTINE BOOKS   NEW YORK

Editor: Sandy Carr
Design: Patrick McLeavey
Fashion photography: Tony Boase
Still life photography: Christine Hanscomb
Detail and flat shot photography: Andrew Haywood
Fashion stylist: Gabi Tubbs
Pattern checker: Marilyn Wilson
Charts: Dennis Hawkins
Illustrations: Connie Jude

Library of Congress Cataloging-in-Publication Data
Duckworth, Susan.
Susan Duckworth's knitting.
Caption title: Susan Duckworth knitting.
1. Knitting – Patterns.   I. Title.   II. Title:
Susan Duckworth knitting.    III. Knitting.
TT820.D769    1988       746.9′2       87-48000
ISBN 0-345-35276-9

Set by Rowland Phototypesetting Ltd,
Bury St Edmunds, Suffolk
Manufactured in Spain

First American Edition: October·1988

10 9 8 7 6 5 4 3 2 1

*Note: The patterns in this book are
not to be knitted for resale.*

*To Jean*

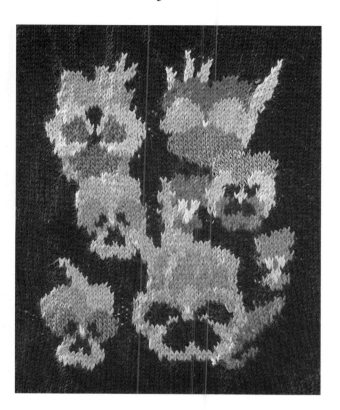

# Contents

*Yarn kits are obtainable for these designs. See page 143 for details.

# Introduction

I have always had a keen interest in all types of craftwork. My grandmother, mother and aunt were all trained painters and teachers, so I was lucky enough to grow up surrounded by strong artistic influences. I spent a few years at art college studying painting, and then I worked for a short while as a make-up artist at BBC Television. But after that I settled down to experiment with knitting.

Knitting is such a rewarding craft – so immediate. Just two knitting needles and a bag of yarn and away you go. Every stitch pattern is based on simple knit one, purl one combinations, and when you add variations by twisting the yarns to the front or back, or working yarn overs, or using cable needles to move blocks of stitches around, wonderful pieces of fabric can be created.

My main interest has been in working from traditional patterns, and recreating them using colour and texture. The relationships and proportions of colours to each other are endlessly intriguing. If you take just those two aspects, the possible developments are infinite, and I can see they will fascinate me throughout my life. When working with colour I think it is important to give yourself a huge range, rather than just a few tones. When I'm designing something, I surround myself with enormous quantities of coloured yarns. Then through a process of building – adding and taking away – and squinting at it all to see the effect, I go into a kind of colour trance until interesting combinations begin to appear – and then the fun begins.

Simple stitch patterns (like stocking stitch) lend themselves to this approach as you can concentrate entirely on the colours if the pattern is not too taxing. But with more intricate patterns I knit up a great many swatches – my working swatches – and Swiss-darn over the colours, rather like over-painting, to get the right balance. I have trunks of these discarded swatches, which are quite as important as the final piece.

When I first began to knit seriously I was absolutely overwhelmed by the limitless possibilities the medium provided. I worked flat out day and night developing stitches found in old books, recolouring, adapting, and working out new shapes. At first I restricted myself to natural and neutral tones – soft, warm browns through to cooler creams. In this way I was concentrating on the stitchcraft, not the colour so much; that came later when I felt more competent. Certainly, designing for knitting provides great scope for using colour in a bold and exciting way – I am not too thrilled by very soft, safe colour combinations such as often appear in furnishing fabrics.

(Right) An appliquéd bird that I made when I was six years old.

(Far right) A detail from the Silver Birch pullover – page 126.

(Below) Winding wool in a corner of my studio in Farnham.

After a period of experiment, when I was luckily able to support myself with freelance make-up work, I joined 401½ workshops, a diverse group of artists and craftspeople. This coincided with the beginning of the knitting 'revival' when there was a great deal of interest in what was happening in hand-knitting design, and overseas buyers flooded into London. Soon I began to acquire a variety of clients: individuals and shops like Browns, Whistles and The Beauchamp Place Shop, and other design companies like Dorothée Bis and Gudule. One of my earliest

commissions was for a seven-foot American footballer, and another was for a dog – a tiny, pampered Yorkshire terrier that lived in Eaton Square. I made it a richly embossed padded and beaded winter jacket – but at the first fitting the poor creature collapsed under the weight!

Many of my early pieces were very intricate, even more so than they are today. I worked sometimes all night to complete them. On several occasions I tried to speed things up by combining hand techniques with machine knitting, but soon found that no machine could cope with the number of colours and variety of textures I wanted to use. For this reason, too, it is virtually impossible to adapt these designs for mass production.

From 401½ workshops I moved into my own studio in Maida Vale in London, and took on assistants and more knitters to make up the growing number of orders. The actual selling of the designs is very interesting and provides an important feedback from buyers, helping to keep the designs moving and developing. But I soon found that I was not interested in running a huge business, especially if this meant spending more of my time on administration, and less on the design side which I love best. About that time, too, I had my first child and the attraction of commuting began to pall. So I had a large workshop built in our garden in Farnham, and that is where I have worked ever since.

Some years ago Hugh Ehrman began using some of my designs for knitting kits, and this was for me a new and very welcome development. I like to think of my sweaters being worn by lots of different people, rather than just hanging in displays and exhibitions, and the kits bring them within reach of anybody with reasonable knitting skills. I very much hope this book will continue that process.

*(Top) Christine's atmospheric picture of baskets full of basketweave swatches – one of my favourite stitches.*

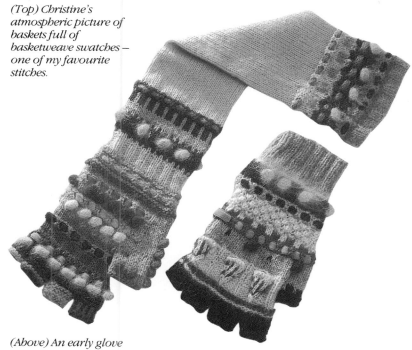

*(Above) An early glove and gauntlet. I was interested in multi-textures at the time, and these were designed to match two short-sleeved sweaters. They use a mixture of yarns and woven velvet ribbons.*

*Susan Duckworth*

# *Wild Roses*

I deliberately chose mohair for this rose design jacket and sweater in order to soften the outlines of the blooms and create a less formal, misty, impressionist flavour.

*(Opposite) The Wild Roses jacket was the last shot of the day, and as the sun went down over Suffolk fields it was flooded with a lovely glow of warm colour.*

□ = A      ⊞ = G
⊡ = B      ☒ = H
◨ = C      ◉ = J
◪ = D      ◨ = L
Ⅵ = E      ◮ = M
◩ = F      ⊟ = N

### SIZE
**Jacket and Sweater**
**To fit** one size up to 101cm (40in) bust
**Actual width measurement** 127cm (50in)
**Length to shoulder** 69cm (27in)
**Sleeve seam** 51cm (20in)

### MATERIALS
**Jacket**
600g (22oz) mohair in main colour (A)
25g (1oz) in each of 11 contrast colours
    (B,C,D,E,F,G,H,J,L,M,N)
**Sweater**
500g (18oz) mohair in main colour (A)
25g (1oz) in each of 15 contrast colours
    (B,C,D,E,F,G,H,J,L,M,N,Q,R,S,T)

1 pair each 3¾mm (US5) and 4mm (US6) needles
1 3¾mm (US5) circular needle (jacket only)
6 buttons (jacket only)

*NOTE: A yarn kit is available for the jacket. See page 143 for details.*

### TENSION
20 sts and 26 rows to 10cm (4in) over patt on 4mm (US6) needles.

## JACKET

### BACK
Using 3¾mm (US5) needles and yarn A, cast on 127 sts. Work 5cm (2in) in K1, P1 rib.
Change to 4mm (US6) needles and work 2.5cm (1in) in st st, ending with a ws row.
Now beg colour patt from chart 1, working in st st throughout and using separate lengths of yarn for each colour area, twisting yarns between colours to avoid holes, as foll:
**1st row** (rs) K9A, (patt 1st row of chart 1) twice, K8A.
**2nd row** P8A, (patt 2nd row of chart 1) twice, P9A.
These 2 rows set the position of chart.
Cont in patt until back measures 45cm (17½in) from cast-on edge, ending with a ws row.
**Shape armholes**
Keeping patt correct, cast off 5 sts at beg of next 4 rows. 107 sts.**
Now work straight until back measures 24cm (9½in) from beg of armhole shaping, ending with a ws row.
**Shape shoulders**
Cast off 11 sts at beg of next 6 rows. Cast off.

### LEFT FRONT
Using 3¾mm (US5) needles and yarn A, cast on 61 sts. Work 5cm (2in) in K1, P1 rib.
Change to 4mm (US6) needles and work 2.5cm (1in) in st st, ending with a ws row.
Now beg colour patt from chart 1 as foll:
**1st row** (rs) K3A, patt 1st row of chart 1, K3A.
**2nd row** P3A, patt 2nd row of chart 1, P3A.
These 2 rows set chart position.
Cont as set until left front matches back to armhole, ending with a ws row.
**Shape armhole**
Cast off 5 sts at beg of next and foll alt row, ending at neck edge. 51 sts.
**Shape neck**
Keeping patt correct, dec 1 st at neck edge on next and every foll 3rd row until 33 sts rem.
Now work straight until left front matches back to shoulder, ending at armhole edge.
**Shape shoulder**
Cast off 11 sts at beg of next and foll alt row. 11 sts.
Work 1 row. Cast off.

### RIGHT FRONT
Work as given for left front, reversing all shapings.

### SLEEVES
Using 3¾mm (US5) needles and yarn A, cast on 40 sts.

CHART 1                                     rep from 1st row

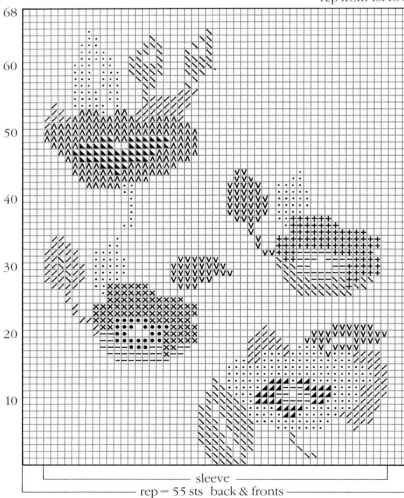

— sleeve —
— rep = 55 sts   back & fronts —

*(Opposite) The Wild Roses sweater is a generously wide shape, but can still look soft and pretty. The pewter grey is particularly flattering to almost any skin tone.*

Work 11cm (4¼in) in K1, P1 rib.
**Next row** (Inc 1, rib 4) to last 5 sts, inc 1, rib 3, inc 1. 49 sts.
Change to 4mm (US6) needles and work 2.5cm (1in) in st st, ending with a ws row.
Now work in colour patt from chart 1 between sleeve markers, *at the same time* inc 1 st at each end of next and every foll 3rd row until there are 107 sts, working the extra sts in yarn A, ending with a ws row.
Now work straight until sleeve measures 51cm (20in) from cast-on edge, ending with a ws row.
**Shape top**
Cast off 5 sts at beg of next 4 rows.
Then dec 1 st at each end of every row until 71 sts rem. Cast off.

## POCKETS (make 2)

Using 3¾mm (US5) needles and yarn A, cast on 31 sts.
Beg with a K row, work 2 rows in st st.
**Next row** Cast on 10 sts, K to end. 41 sts.
Cont in st st, dec 1 st at beg (top edge) of next and every foll alt row until there are 25 sts, ending with a P row. Work 4 rows straight.
Now inc 1 st at end (top edge) of next and every foll alt row until there are 41 sts, ending with a P row.
**Next row** Cast off 10 sts, K to end. 31 sts.
P 1 row.
Cast off.

## COLLAR

Using 3¾mm (US5) circular needle and yarn A, cast on 156 sts. Work 30 rows in K1, P1 rib, *at the same time* dec 1 st at each end of every row. 96 sts.
Cast off in rib.

| | | |
|---|---|---|
| □ = A | ⊡ = J | |
| ⊡ = B | ◩ = L | |
| ◨ = C | ☒ = M | |
| ⊡ = D | ◉ = N | |
| ▽ = E | ◪ = Q | |
| ▲ = F | ◸ = R | |
| ◥ = G | ⊟ = S | |
| ⊞ = H | ◫ = T | |

CHART 2                                    rep from 1st row

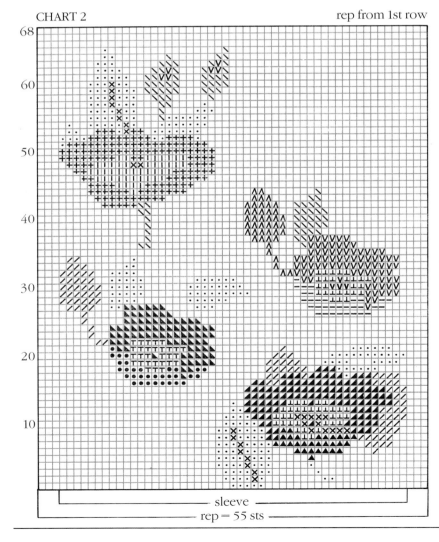

— sleeve —
rep = 55 sts

## BUTTON BAND

Using 3¾mm (US5) needles and yarn A, cast on 11 sts.
Work in K1, P1 rib until band when slightly stretched fits up left front edge to 3cm (1¼in) below beg of neck shaping.
**Top shaping**
Work 2 tog at inner edge on next 7 rows. 4 sts.
**Next row** (K2 tog) twice.
Fasten off.
Mark positions of 6 buttons, one 1cm (½in) from cast-on edge, one 1cm (½in) from cast-off edge and the rest spaced evenly between.

## BUTTONHOLE BAND

Work to match button band, reversing top shaping, making buttonholes to correspond with button markers as foll:
**1st buttonhole row** (rs) Rib 3, cast off 3 sts, rib to end.
**2nd buttonhole row** Rib to end, casting on 3 sts over those cast off in previous row.

## TO MAKE UP

Join shoulder seams.
Join on button and buttonhole bands to beg of neck shaping, stretching slightly to fit.
Join on cast-off edge of collar to neck edge and top of front bands.
Set in sleeves.
Fold pocket linings in half, rs tog, and join shaped edges.
Pin linings in position with cast-on and cast-off edges at side seams.
Join sleeve seams, side seams and edges of pocket openings.
Sew on buttons.

# SWEATER

## BACK

Work as given for jacket back, foll chart 2 instead of chart 1.

## FRONT

Work as given for back to **.
Now work straight until front measures 18cm (7in) from beg of armhole shaping, ending with a ws row.
**Divide for neck**
**Next row** Patt 45 sts, turn, leaving rem sts on a spare needle, and cont on these sts only for first side of neck.
Dec 1 st at neck edge on every row until 33 sts rem.
Now work straight until front matches back to shoulder, ending at armhole edge.
**Shape shoulder**
Cast off 11 sts at beg of next and foll alt row.
Work 1 row. Cast off rem 11 sts.
With rs of work facing, return to sts on spare needle, rejoin yarn to next st, cast off centre 17 sts, patt to end. 45 sts. Complete second side of neck to match first side, reversing shapings.

## SLEEVES

Work as given for jacket, foll chart 2 instead of chart 1.

## TO MAKE UP

Join right shoulder seam.
**Collar**
With rs of work facing, using 3¾mm (US5) needles and yarn A, K up 108 sts evenly around neck edge.
Work 10cm (4in) in K1 tbl, P1 rib.
Cast off in rib.
Join left shoulder and collar seam.
Set in sleeves flat, matching centre of cast-off edge to shoulder seam. Join side and sleeve seams.

# *Moths*

The tweedy, blue wool has a real feeling of a night sky, against which a cloud of softly coloured moths provide a delicate contrast.

## SIZE
**To fit** one size up to 101cm (40in) bust
**Actual width measurement** 106cm (41¾in)
**Length to shoulder** 71cm (28in)
**Sleeve seam** 48cm (18¾in)

## MATERIALS
350g (12½oz) Rowan Fine Fleck Tweed in blue tweed 97 (A)

25g (1oz) each in rose tweed 410 (C) and gold tweed 14 (N)
25g (1oz) Rowan Botany Wool each in lavender 59 (B), loden 89 (D), red rust 77 (E), bark 82 (F), turquoise 633 (G), navy 97 (H), candy 95 (J), ginger 78 (M), bright buddleia 501 (Q), rose 637 (R), dove 52 (S), olive 60 (T), dull buddleia 127 (U) and grape 59 (V)
25g (1oz) Rowan Lightweight Double Knitting in deep lilac 93 (L)
**Equivalent yarn** four-ply
1 pair each 3mm (US2) and 3¼mm (US3) needles

*NOTE: A yarn kit is available for this design. See page 143 for details.*

## TENSION
25 sts and 35 rows to 10cm (4in) over st st on 3¼mm (US3) needles.

## BACK
Using 3mm (US2) needles and yarn A, cast on 151 sts. Work 18cm (7in) in K1, P1 rib.
Change to 3¼mm (US3) needles and beg colour patt from chart, working in st st throughout and using separate lengths of yarn for each colour area, twisting yarns tog at colour joins to avoid holes, as foll:
**1st row** (rs) K11A, (patt 1st row of chart) 3 times, K11A.
**2nd row** P11A, (patt 2nd row of chart) 3 times, P11A.
These 2 rows set the position of chart.
Cont as set until back measures 46cm (18in) from cast-on edge, ending with a ws row.
**Shape armholes**
Keeping patt correct, cast off 8 sts at beg of next 2 rows. 135 sts.\*\*
Now work straight until back measures 25cm (10in) from beg of armhole shaping ending with a ws row (when chart has been worked twice, cont in yarn A only).
**Shape shoulders**
Cast off 14 sts at beg of next 6 rows.
Cast off rem 51 sts.

## FRONT
Work as given for back to \*\*.
Now work straight until front measures 14 rows less than back to shoulder shaping ending with a ws row (when chart has been worked twice, cont in yarn A only).
**Divide for neck**
**Next row** Patt 54 sts, turn, leaving rem sts on a spare needle and cont on these sts only for first side of neck. Dec 1 st at neck edge on every row until 42 sts rem. Now work straight until front matches back to shoulder, ending at armhole edge.
**Shape shoulder**
Cast off 14 sts at beg of next and foll alt row. 15 sts. Work 1 row. Cast off.
With rs of work facing, return to sts on spare needle. Rejoin yarn to next st, cast off centre 35 sts, patt to end. 50 sts.
Complete to match first side of neck, reversing shapings.

rep 1st – 84th rows

84
80

70

60

50

40

30

20

10

rep = 43 sts

□ = A
☑ = B
⊡ = C
◉ = D
◪ = E
⊡ = F
☒ = G
◥ = H
▽ = J
◩ = L
◤ = M
◣ = N
⊞ = Q
⊟ = R
⊞ = S
◹ = T
⊤ = U
◩ = V

*These two make a satisfying contrast – the strong, angular Kimono (see page 68) sets off the pullover with its gentle scattering of moths.*

## SLEEVES

Using 3mm (US2) needles and yarn A, cast on 64 sts.
Work 12cm (4½in) in K1, P1 rib.
**Next row** K1, P1, (K into front and back of next st, P1) to end. 95 sts.
Change to 3¼mm (US3) needles and beg colour patt from chart as foll:
**1st row** (rs) K26A, patt 1st row of chart, K26A.
**2nd row** P26A, patt 2nd row of chart, P26A.
These 2 rows set the position of chart.
Cont as set, *at the same time* inc 1 st at each end of next and every foll 3rd row until there are 131 sts, working the extra sts in yarn A.
Now work straight until 122 rows have been worked from chart, then cont in yarn A only until sleeve measures 51cm (20in) from cast-on edge, ending with a ws row. Cast off.

## COLLAR

Using 3mm (US2) needles and yarn A, cast on 148 sts.

Work in basketweave st as foll:
**1st row** (rs) K4, (P4, K4) to end.
**2nd row** P4, (K4, P4) to end.
**3rd–4th rows** As 1st–2nd rows.
**5th row** As 2nd row.
**6th row** As 1st row.
**7th–8th rows** As 5th–6th rows.
These 8 rows form the patt rep.
Cont in basketweave st until collar measures 8cm (3in). Now work 6 rows in K1, P1 rib.
Cast off in rib.

## TO MAKE UP

Join shoulder seams.
Join on collar, matching centre of cast-off edge to centre back, and both edges to centre front.
Set in sleeves flat, matching centre of cast-off edge to shoulder seam, and joining last few rows of sleeve to cast-off sts at underarm.
Join side and sleeve seams.

# Pansies

Pansies are some of my favourite flowers. Last summer, when working on this design, I indulged myself and filled my garden with every possible variety. I'm longing to work this one in darker tones in wools and velvety chenilles. The cotton version is in glowing, sunny colours.

## SIZE

**To fit** one size only up to 101cm (40in) bust
**Actual width measurement** 111cm (43¾in)
**Length to shoulder** 70cm (27½in)
**Sleeve seam** 53cm (21in)

## MATERIALS

400g (15oz) Rowan Yarns Sea Breeze Soft Cotton in rain cloud 528 (A)
50g (2oz) each in antique pink 533 (B), sugar pink 545 (C), balze 540 (D), purple 543 (E), sienna 535 (F), strawberry ice 546 (G), frolic 534 (H), apple 537 (J), wheat 523 (L), bluebell 542 (M), black 526 (N), spring yellow 536 (Q) and lilac 544 (R)
50g (2oz) Rowan Cabled Mercerised Cotton each in jettison 310 (S), cadmium 304 (T), lavender 311 (U), terracotta 314 (V) and puce 315 (W)
**Equivalent yarn** four-ply
1 pair each 3mm (US2) and 3¼mm (US3) needles
Cable needle and 10 buttons

*NOTE: A yarn kit is available for this design. See page 143 for details.*

## TENSION

30 sts and 35 rows to 10cm (4in) over patt on 3¼mm (US3) needles.

## SPECIAL ABBREVIATION

*cable 8* – sl next 4 sts on to a cable needle and hold at front of work, K4, then K4 from cable needle

## BACK

Using 3¼mm (US3) needles and yarn A, cast on 116 sts. Work in K1 tbl, P1 rib, *at the same time* cast on 4 sts at beg of next 8 rows, then 2 sts at beg of foll 10 rows. ending with a ws row. 168 sts.
**Next row** Rib 24, K to last 24 sts, rib 24.
**Next row** Rib 22, P to last 22 sts, rib 22.
**Next row** Rib 20, K to last 20 sts, rib 20.
Cont in this way, working 2 fewer sts in rib at each side, and 4 more sts in st st in the centre panel, on every row until the row 'Rib 10, P to last 10 sts, rib 10 has been worked.
Now beg colour patt from chart, using separate lengths of yarn for each colour area, and twisting yarns tog at colour joins to avoid holes, as foll:
**1st row** (rs) Rib 9A, K16A, (patt 1st row of chart) twice, K16A, rib 9A.
**2nd row** Rib 8A, P17A, (patt 2nd row of chart) twice P17A, rib 8A.
**3rd row** Rib 7A, K18A, (patt 3rd row of chart) twice, K18A, rib 7A.
**4th row** Rib 6A, P19A, (patt 4th row of chart) twice, P19A, rib 6A. These 4 rows set chart position.

Cont as set, working 1 st less in rib and 1 st more in st st at each side on every row until all sts are worked in st st. Cont in chart patt until back measures 46cm (18¼in) from cast-on edge, ending with a ws row.

**Shape armholes**

Cast off 8 sts at beg of next 2 rows, then dec 1 st at each end of foll 4 alt rows. 144 sts.

Now work straight until back measures 24cm (9½in) from beg of armhole shaping, ending with a ws row. Cast off.

**LEFT FRONT**

Using 3¼mm (US3) needles and yarn A, cast on 53 sts. Work in K1 tbl, P1 rib, *at the same time* cast on 4 sts at beg of next and foll 3 alt rows, then 2 sts at beg of foll 5 rows ending with a ws row. 79 sts.

**Next row** Rib 24, K to end.

**Next row** P to last 22 sts, rib 22.

Cont in this way, work 2 fewer sts in rib at right-hand (side) edge on each row until the row 'P to last 10 sts, rib 10' has been worked.

Now beg colour patt from chart as foll:

**1st row** (rs) Rib 9A, K6A, patt 1st row of chart, K5A.

**2nd row** P5A, patt 2nd row of chart, P7A, rib 8A.

These 2 rows set chart patt.

Cont as set working 1 st less in rib at right-hand side until all sts are in st st.

Now cont in patt until left front matches back to armhole, ending with a ws row.

**Shape armhole**

Cast off 8 sts at beg of next row, then dec 1 st at beg of foll 4 alt rows. 67 sts. Now work straight until left front measures 19cm (7½in) from beg of armhole shaping, ending at neck edge.

**Shape neck**

Cast off 13 sts at beg of next row, then 2 sts at beg of every foll alt row until 44 sts rem.

Work straight until left front matches back to cast-off edge.

Cast off.

**RIGHT FRONT**

Work as given for left front, reversing ribbed edging, chart position and all shapings.

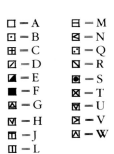

| | | | |
|---|---|---|---|
| □ = A | ⊟ = M | | |
| ⊡ = B | ⊠ = N | | |
| ⊞ = C | ⊡ = Q | | |
| ◪ = D | ◩ = R | | |
| ◨ = E | ◉ = S | | |
| ■ = F | ⊠ = T | | |
| ◩ = G | ◩ = U | | |
| ◪ = H | ▷ = V | | |
| ◫ = J | ◩ = W | | |
| ◫ = L | | | |

rep from 1st row

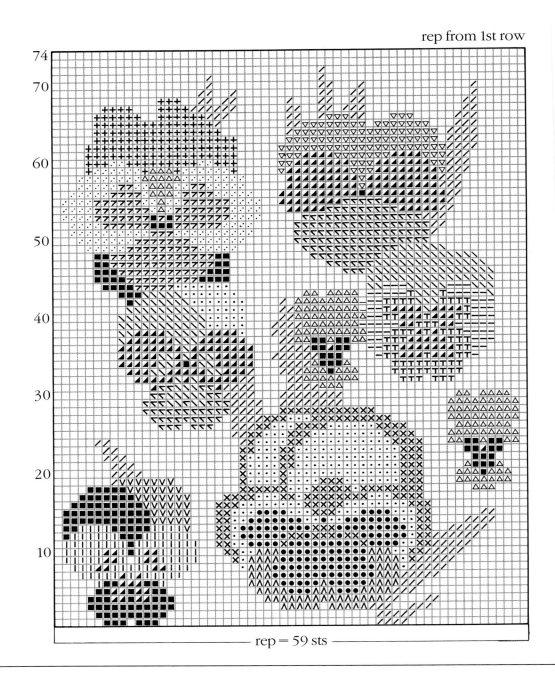

74
70
60
50
40
30
20
10

rep = 59 sts

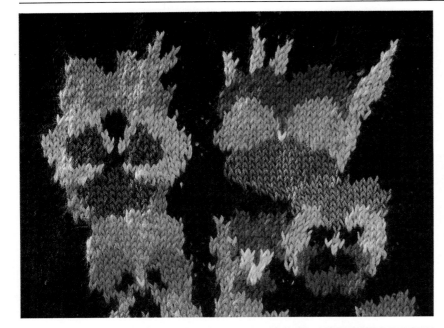

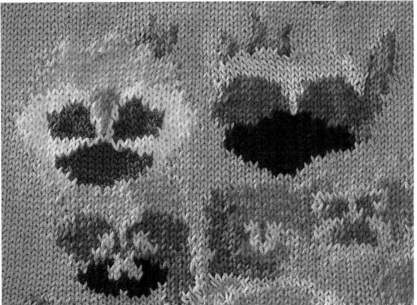

*I've had a lot of fun with the Pansies design, and here are some of the results. Surprisingly, the only difference between the blue and cream colourways is the background colour – the pansies are identical. Sometimes I make it in wool instead of cotton as in the bilberry colourway (opposite).*

## SLEEVES

Using 3¼mm (US3) needles and yarn A, cast on 71 sts.
Work in colour patt from chart as foll:
**1st row** (rs) K6A, patt 1st row of chart, K6A.
**2nd row** P6A, patt 2nd row of chart, P6A.
These 2 rows set chart position.
Cont in patt as set, *at the same time* inc 1 st at each end of next and every foll 5th row until there are 81 sts, then of every foll 3rd row until there are 149 sts.
Now work straight until 148 rows have been worked in chart patt.
**Shape top**
Cast off 8 sts at beg of next 2 rows, then dec 1 st at each end of foll 4 alt rows. 125 sts.
Cast off.

## CUFFS

With rs of work facing, using 3¼mm (US3) needles and yarn A, K up 82 sts evenly along lower sleeve edge.
Work in cable patt as foll:
**1st and every alt row** (ws) K2, (P8, K2) to end.
**2nd row** P2, (K8, P2) to end.
**4th row** P2, (cable 8, P2) to end.
**6th and 8th rows** P2, (K8, P2) to end.

These 8 rows form the cable patt.
Cont in cable patt until cuff measures 11.5cm (4½in) from K-up row, ending with a ws row.
Change to 3mm (US2) needles and work 12 rows in K1 tbl, P1 rib.
Cast off in rib.

## COLLAR

Using 3¼mm (US3) needles and yarn A, cast 152 sts.
Work in cable patt as for cuff until collar measures 6.5cm (2½in) from cast-on edge.
Change to 3mm (US2) needles and work 5 rows in K1 tbl, P1 rib.
Cast off in rib.

## COLLAR EDGINGS

With rs of work facing, using 3mm (US2) needles and yarn A, K up 24 sts evenly along row-ends edge of collar.
Work 5 rows in K1 tbl, P1 rib.
Cast off in rib.
Work a similar edging on opposite side of collar.

## BUTTON BAND

Using 3mm (US2) needles and yarn A, cast on 11 sts.
Work in K1 tbl, P1 rib until band when slightly stretched fits smoothly up left front edge to beg of neck shaping.
Cast off in rib.
Mark positions of 10 buttons, one 2cm (¾in) from cast-on edge, one 2cm (¾in) from cast-off edge, and the rest spaced evenly between.

## BUTTONHOLE BAND

Work as given for button band, making buttonholes to correspond with button markers as foll:
**1st buttonhole row** (rs) Rib 4, cast off 3 sts, rib to end.
**2nd buttonhole row** Rib to end, casting on 3 sts over those cast off in previous row.

## TO MAKE UP

Join shoulder seams.
Join on button and buttonhole bands.
Join cast-on edge of collar to neck edge and tops of front bands.
Set in sleeves, matching centre of cast-off edge to shoulder seam.
Join side and sleeve seams.
Sew on buttons.

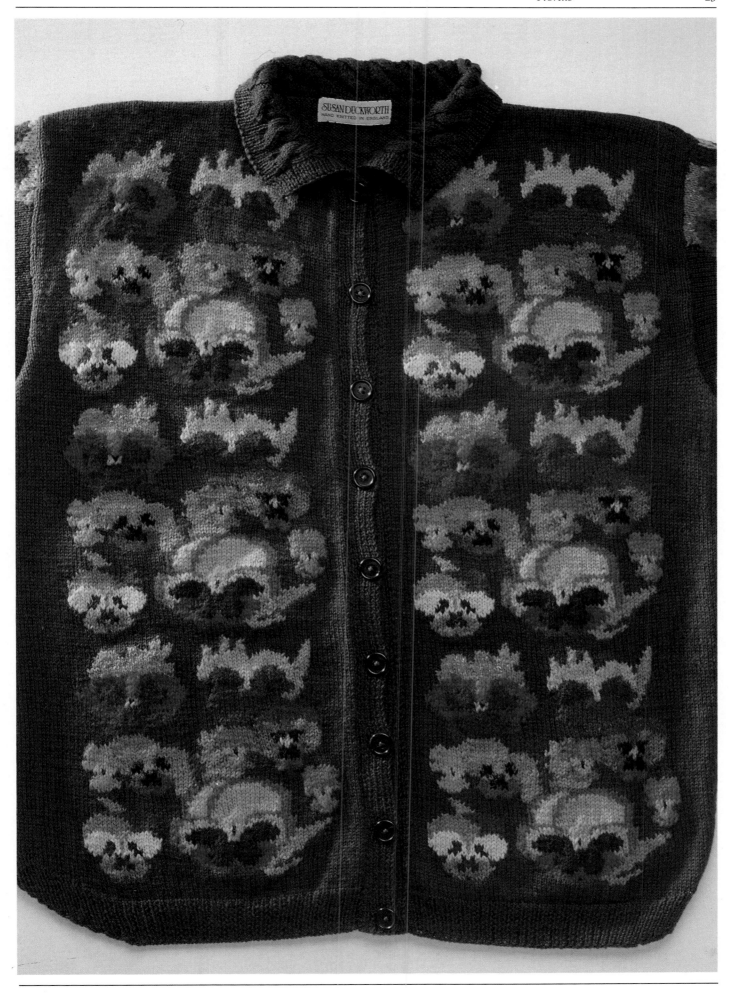

# *Blackwork*

I found some superb examples of 16th-century Spanish blackwork embroidery, and adapted them for this pullover and cardigan. The original embroideries used a white background, of course, but I hardly ever use white in my work. I find it harsh.

### SIZES
To fit 91[96]cm (36[38]in) bust
**Sweater**
**Actual width measurements** 96[101]cm (38[40]in)
**Length to shoulder** 69cm (27in)
**Sleeve seam** 51cm (20in)
**Cardigan**
**Actual width measurements** 95[100]cm (37½[39½]in)
**Length to shoulder** 57cm (22½in)
**Sleeve seam** 43cm (17in) including frill

### MATERIALS
**Sweater**
450[500]g (17[19]oz) Rowan Cabled Mercerised
   Cotton in ecru 301 (A)
200g (8oz) in black 319 (B)
**Cardigan**
450[500]g (17[19]oz) in black 319 (A)
200g (8oz) in ecru 301 (B)
**Equivalent yarn** four-ply
1 pair each 3mm (US2) and 3¼mm (US3) needles
3mm (US2) circular needle
7 buttons (cardigan only)

*NOTE: A yarn kit is available for the cardigan. See page 143 for details.*

### TENSION
30 sts and 34 rows to 10cm (4in) over patt on 3¼mm (US3) needles.

## SWEATER

### BACK
Using 3mm (US2) needles and yarn A, cast on 144[152] sts.
Work 15.5cm (6in) in K1 tbl, P1 rib.
Change to 3¼mm (US3) needles and beg colour patt from chart, working in st st throughout, strand yarn A loosely across back of work but use separate lengths of yarn B for each motif, twisting yarns tog at colour joins to avoid holes(do not work parts of motifs at sides of work).
Cont in patt until back measures 46cm (18in) from cast-on edge, ending with a ws row.
**Shape armholes**
Cast off 8 sts at beg of next 2 rows. 128[136] sts.**
Now work straight until back measures 23cm (9in) from beg of armhole shaping) ending with a ws row.
**Shape shoulders**
Cast off 13[14] sts at beg of next 4 rows, and 13[15] sts at beg of foll 2 rows.
Cast off rem 50 sts.

### FRONT
Work as given for back to **

□ = A
☒ = B

cardigan right front 2nd size
cardigan left front 2nd size
cardigan fronts 1st size

sweater sleeves
cardigan sleeves
1st size back
2nd size back

cardigan right front 2nd size
cardigan left front 2nd size
cardigan fronts 1st size

rep 1st–106th rows

sweater sleeves
cardigan sleeves
1st size back
2nd size back

Now work straight until front measures 14 rows less than back to shoulder shaping, ending with a ws row.

**Divide for neck**

**Next row** Patt 50[54] sts, turn, leaving rem sts on a spare needle, and cont on these sts only for first side of neck.

Now dec 1 st at neck edge on every row until 39[43] sts rem. Work straight until front matches back to shoulder, ending at armhole edge.

**Shape shoulder**

Cast off 13[14] sts at beg of next and foll alt row.

Work 1 row.

Cast off rem 13[15] sts.

With rs of work facing, return to sts on spare needle, rejoin yarn to next st, cast off centre 28 sts, patt to end. 50[54] sts.

Complete second side of neck to match first side reversing shaping.

## CUFF FRILL (make 2)

Using 3mm (US2) circular needle and yarn B, cast on 116 sts. Work in rows.

Work bell edging as foll:

**1st row** (rs) P2, (K7, P7) to last 2 sts, P2.
**2nd row** K2, (K7, P7) to last 2 sts, K2.
**3rd row** P2, (K2 tog tbl, K3, K2 tog, P7) to last 2 sts, P2.
**4th row** K2, (K7, P5) to last 2 sts, K2.
**5th row** P2, (K2 tog tbl, K1, K2 tog, P7) to last 2 sts, P2.
**6th row** K2, (K7, P3) to last 2 sts, K2.
**7th row** P2, (sl 1, K2 tog tbl, psso, P7) to last 2 sts, P2.
**8th row** K2, (K7, P1) to last 2 sts, K2.
**9th row** P2, (K2 tog tbl, P6) to last 2 sts, P2.
**10th row** K2, (K6, P1) to last 2 sts, K2. 60 sts.

Change to yarn A.

K 1 row. Leave these sts on a spare needle.

## SLEEVES

Using 3mm (US2) needles and yarn A, cast on 60 sts. Work 13cm (5in) in K1 tbl, P1 rib.

Now graft cuff frill on to sleeve as foll:

**Next row** With rs of work facing, place spare needle holding frill in front of left-hand needle and, using yarn A, K tog one st from each needle to end. 60 sts.

Change to 3¼mm (US3) needles.

**Next row** (P1, P twice into next st) to end. 90 sts.

Now beg colour patt from chart, working between sleeve markers, *at the same time* inc 1 st at each end of every foll 3rd row until there are 140 sts (do not work part motifs at sides of work).

Work straight until sleeve measures 53.5cm (21in) from cast-on edge. Cast off.

## NECK FRILL

Using 3mm (US2) circular needle and yarn B, cast on 242 sts.

Work 10 rows in bell edging as given for cuff frill. 123 sts. Leave these sts on a spare needle.

## TO MAKE UP

Join right shoulder seam.

**Neck band**

With rs of work facing, using 3mm (US2) needles and yarn A, K up 73 sts evenly around front neck edge, and 50 sts across back neck. 123 sts.

Break yarn and transfer sts to spare needle so that next row can be worked with rs facing.

Graft neck frill on to neck edge as given for cuff frill. 123 sts.

Now work 5 rows in K1 tbl, P1 rib.

Cast off in rib.

Join left shoulder, neckband seam and frill seam.

Set in sleeves flat, matching centre of cast-off edge to shoulder seam, and sewing last few rows of sleeve to cast-off sts at underarm.

Join side and sleeve seams.

# CARDIGAN

## BACK
Using 3mm (US2) needles and yarn A, cast on 144[152] sts.
Work 6cm (2½in) in K1 tbl, P1 rib.
Change to 3¼mm (US3) needles and work 100 rows in colour patt from chart as given for back of sweater, ending with a ws row.
### Shape armholes
Cast off 8 sts at beg of next 2 rows.
Now dec 1 st at each end of next and every foll alt row until 104[112] sts rem.
Now work straight until back measures 22cm (8½in) from beg of armhole shaping, ending with a ws row.
### Shape shoulders
Cast off 9[11] sts at beg of next 2 rows, then 9[10] sts at beg of foll 4 rows.
Cast off rem 50 sts.

## LEFT FRONT
Using 3mm (US2) needles and yarn A, cast on 67[71] sts.
Work as given for back to armhole, working from chart between left front markers, ending with a ws row.
### Shape armhole
Cast off 8 sts at beg of next row, then dec 1 st at armhole edge on 12 foll alt rows. 47[51] sts.
Now work straight until front measures 18cm (7in) from beg of armhole shaping, ending with a rs row.
### Shape neck
Cast off 10 sts at beg of next row, then cast off 2 sts at neck edge on every alt row until 27[31] sts rem.
Now work straight until front matches back to shoulder, ending at armhole edge.
### Shape shoulder
Cast off 9[11] sts at beg of next row, then 9[10] sts at beg of foll alt row.
Work 1 row.
Cast off rem 9[10] sts.

## RIGHT FRONT
Work as given for left front, working between left front chart markers, and reversing shapings.

## SLEEVES
Using 3mm (US2) needles and yarn B, cast on 116 sts.
Work 10 rows in bell edging as given for sweater cuff frill. 60 sts.
Change to yarn A.
K 1 row (rs).
Now work 11cm (4¼in) in K1 tbl, P1 rib, ending with a rs row.
Change to 3¼mm (US3) needles.
**Next row** P4, (P1, inc 1 P-wise into each of next 3 sts) to last 4 sts, P4. 99 sts.
Now work 100 rows in colour patt from chart, working between cardigan sleeve markers.
### Shape top
Cast off 3 sts at beg of next 6 rows, then 2 sts at beg of foll 4 rows.
Now dec 1 st at each end of every row until 67 sts rem, then of every alt row until 57 sts rem. Then dec 1 st at each end of every 3rd row until 41 sts rem.
Now cast off 6 sts at beg of next 4 rows.
Cast off rem 17 sts.

## BUTTON BAND
Using 3mm (US2) needles and yarn A, cast on 11 sts.
Work in K1 tbl, P1 rib until band when slightly stretched fits up left front opening edge, ending with a ws row.
Leave these sts on a safety pin.
Mark positions for 7 buttons, one 1cm (½in) from

cast-on edge, one 1cm (½in) from top edge and the rest spaced evenly between.

## BUTTONHOLE BAND
Work as given for button band, making buttonholes to correspond with button markers as foll:
**1st buttonhole row** (rs) Rib 4, cast off 3 sts, rib to end.
**2nd buttonhole row** Rib to end, casting on 3 sts over those cast off in previous row.

## NECK FRILL
Work as given for sweater neck frill.

## TO MAKE UP
Join shoulder seams.
Join on button and buttonhole bands.
### Neckband
Using 3mm (US2) needles and yarn A, K across 11 sts of buttonhole band, then K up 112 sts evenly around neck edge to inner edge of button band. 123 sts.
Now graft 123 sts of neck frill to first sts of neckband as given for sweater neck frill, then rib last 11 sts of button band. 134 sts.
Cont in K1 tbl, P1 rib, work 7 rows, *at the same time* dec 1 st at each end of next and 3 foll alt rows. 126 sts.
Cast off in rib.
Join side and sleeve seams.
Set in sleeves.
Sew on buttons.

*There is a sweater and cardigan version of this design. Both are easy to knit (only two colours!) and very feminine, edged with soft frills on cuffs on neck.*

# *Camellia*

I wanted this design to be quite simple to knit, so these are fairly stylized camellias! And the yarn is double knitting. I prefer the basketweave background to be worked right into the flower heads, but some people may find it easier to surround them with stocking stitch.

### SIZE
**To fit** one size up to 106cm (42in) bust
**Actual width measurement** 130cm (51in)
**Length to shoulder** 72cm (28¼in)
**Sleeve seam** 51cm (20in)

### MATERIALS
950g (34oz) double-knitting cotton in main colour (A)
50g (2oz) in each of 8 contrast colours (B,C,D,E,F,G,H,J)
25g (1oz) in each of 5 contrast colours (L,M,N,Q,R)
1 pair each 3¼mm (US3) and 3¾mm (US5) needles
6 buttons

### TENSION
20 sts and 28 rows to 10cm (4in) over basketweave patt on 3¾mm (US5) needles.

### POCKET LINING
Using 3¾mm (US5) needles and yarn A, cast on 45 sts.

Work 23cm (9in) in st st, ending with a P row.
Leave these sts on a spare needle.

### FRONT
Using 3¼mm (US3) needles and yarn A, cast on 130 sts. Work 5cm (2in) in K1, P1 rib.**
Change to 3¾mm (US5) needles and work in basketweave patt as foll:
**1st–4th rows** K1, (K4, P4) to last st, K1.
**5th–8th rows** K1, (P4, K4) to last st, K1.
These 8 rows form basketweave patt.
(Note: basketweave patt is worked in A throughout.)
Rep these 8 rows twice more, then 1st–4th rows again.
Now beg floral patt from motif chart, working in st st unless otherwise indicated, and using separate lengths of yarn for each colour area, twisting yarns tog at colour joins to avoid holes, as foll:
**1st row** (rs) Patt 1st row of motif 1 chart, work 20 sts in basketweave patt in yarn A, patt 1st row of motif 1 chart.
This row sets the position of floral motifs; cont in patt as set until 60 rows of motif chart have been completed, thus ending with a ws row.
**Place pocket**
**Next row** Work 5 sts in basketweave patt in yarn A beg 1st row, sl next 45 sts on a stitch holder for pocket top, work in basketweave patt across 45 sts of pocket lining, and to end of row.
Work 3 more rows in basketweave patt.
**Next row** Work 55 sts in basketweave patt, patt 1st row of motif 2 chart, work 20 sts in basketweave patt.
This row sets position of motif 2. Cont as set, work 7 more rows, ending with a ws row.
**Divide for front opening**
**Next row** Work 55 sts in basketweave patt, turn, leaving rem sts on a spare needle, and cont on these sts only for first side of front.
Cont in basketweave patt, work straight until 93 rows have been worked from pocket opening, ending with a rs row.
**Shape neck**
Cast off 10 sts at beg of next row, then 2 sts at beg of foll 3 alt rows. 39 sts. (100 rows have been worked from pocket opening.) Cast off.
With rs of work facing, return to sts on spare needle, rejoin yarn to next st and, keeping motif and basketweave patt correct, work 80 rows straight, ending at front opening.
**Shape neck**
Cast off 15 sts at beg of next row, then 2 sts at beg of foll 3 alt rows. 54 sts.
Now work 1 row straight. Cast off.

### BACK
Work as given for front to **.
Change to 3¾mm (US5) needles.
***Next row** (rs) Work 50 sts in basketweave patt, patt 1st row of motif 1 chart, work in basketweave to end.
This row sets position of motif 1 chart, cont as set until 60 rows of motif chart have been completed.***
Work 2 rows in basketweave patt, end with a ws row.

(Overleaf) *A winter version of the Camellia design worked in wool and angora.*

### MOTIF CHART 1(2)

Note: Colours are given for motif 1 first, with those for motif 2 in brackets.
Work in st st unless otherwise indicated

☑ = A
■ = G on motif 1, Q on motif 2
☒ = M on motif 1, E on motif 2

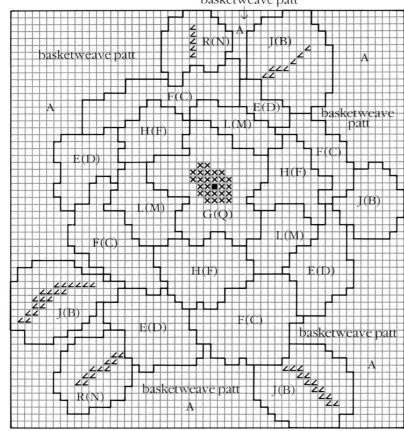

basketweave patt

basketweave patt

A

R(N)   J(B)   A

F(C)

E(D)

H(F)   L(M)   basketweave patt

E(D)

F(C)

H(F)

L(M)

G(Q)

L(M)

F(C)

J(B)

H(F)   E(D)

J(B)

E(D)   F(C)   basketweave patt

R(N)   basketweave patt   J(B)   A

A

**Next row** Work 25 sts in basketweave patt, patt 1st row of motif 2 chart, work in basketweave patt to end.
This row sets position of motif 2 chart; cont as set until 60 rows of motif chart have been completed.
Work 2 rows in basketweave patt, ending with a ws row. Rep from *** to ***.
Now work 4 rows straight.
Cast off.

## SLEEVES

Using 3¼mm (US3) needles and yarn A, cast on 38 sts.
Work 7.5cm (3in) in K1, P1 rib.
**Next row** Rib 1, (rib twice into next st) to last st, rib 1.
74 sts.
Change to 3¾mm (US5) needles and work in basketweave patt as given for front, *at the same time* inc 1 st at each end of next and every foll 3rd row until there are 94 sts, ending with a ws row.
**Next row** Work 19 sts in basketweave patt, patt 1st row of motif 2 chart, work 20 sts in basketweave patt.
This row sets position of motif chart; cont as set, *at the same time* inc on every 3rd row as before until there are 106 sts (when motif chart is complete, cont in basketweave patt only).
Now work straight until sleeve measures 51cm (20in) from cast-on edge.
Cast off.

## POCKET TOP

Using 3¼mm (US3) needles and yarn A, rejoin yarn to 45 sts left on spare needle.
Work 2 rows in K1, P1 rib.
**1st buttonhole row** Rib 21 sts, cast off 3 sts, rib to end.
**2nd buttonhole row** Rib to end, casting on 3 sts over those cast off in previous row.
Rib 2 rows.
Cast off in rib.

## FRONT BAND

Using 3¼mm (US3) needles and yarn A, K up 62 sts evenly along right front opening edge.
Work 3 rows in K1, P1 rib.
**1st buttonhole row** Rib 1, (cast off 3, rib 11 including st used to cast off) 4 times, cast off 3, rib 2.
**2nd buttonhole row** Rib to end, casting on 3 sts over those cast off in previous row.
Rib 3 rows.
Cast off in rib.

## COLLAR

Using 3¼mm (US3) needles and yarn A, cast on 100 sts.
Work in basketweave patt as foll:
**1st and 3rd rows** (rs) K4, (P4, K4) to end.
**2nd and 4th rows** P4, (K4, P4) to end.
**5th and 7th rows** As 2nd and 4th rows.
**6th and 8th rows** As 1st and 3rd rows.
These 8 rows form basketweave patt.
Rep these 8 rows once more, then 1st–4th rows again.
Work 4 rows in K1, P1 rib.
Cast off in rib.

## TO MAKE UP

Join shoulder seams.
Join on collar to neck edge, beg at inner edge of front band, and ending 2.5cm (1in) in from left front opening. Set sleeves in flat, matching centre of cast-off edge to shoulder seam.
Catch down pocket lining on ws and pocket tops on rs. Join side and sleeve seams.
Catch down base of front band.
Sew on buttons.

*On the pink version of Camellia the chart area is worked entirely in stocking stitch.*

# *Long and Short Cables*

The stitch is based on a well-known cable, but I've developed it using colour and pattern. In this version of it the colours in the cables and twists echo the tiny specks and flecks in the tweedy moss-stitch background.

## SIZE
**To fit** one size only up to 101cm (40in)
**Actual width measurement** 114.5cm (45in)
**Length to shoulder** 67cm (26½in)
**Sleeve seam** 43cm (17in)

## MATERIALS
450g (16oz) four-ply wool in main colour (A)
75g (3oz) in each of 6 contrast colours (B,C,D,E,F,G)
25g (1oz) in each of 5 contrast colours (H,J,L,M,N)
1 pair each 2¾mm (US2) and 3¼mm (US3) needles
8 buttons

## TENSION
25 sts and 42 rows to 10cm (4in) over moss st on 3¼mm (US3) needles.
112-st long and short cable patt measures 24cm (9½in) unstretched.

## SPECIAL ABBREVIATIONS
*make 1* – pick up loop between last st and next st and K it tbl
*cn* – cable needle
*cable 8* – sl next 4 sts on to cn and hold at front of work, K4, then K4 from cn

## LEFT FRONT
Using 2¾mm (US2) needles and yarn A, cast on 58 sts.
Work in K2 tbl, P2 rib as foll:
**1st row** (rs) K2 tbl, (P2, K2 tbl) to end.
**2nd row** P2, (K2 tbl, P2) to end.
Rep these 2 rows until work measures 10cm (4in) from cast-on edge, ending with a ws row.
**Next row** (rs) Rib 2, (rib twice into next st) to last 2 sts, rib 2. 112 sts.
Change to 3¼mm (US3) needles. P 1 row.
Now beg long and short cable patt, using separate lengths of yarn for each colour area, twisting yarns tog at colour joins to avoid holes (work in yarn A unless otherwise indicated), as foll:
**1st row** (rs) *P2, K8, P2, K1, K11B, K1, P2, K8, P2, K1, K11C, K1; rep from * once more, P2, K8, P2.
**2nd and every alt row to 22nd row** Using the same colours, K all the P sts of previous row, and P all the K sts.
**3rd row** As 1st row.
**5th row** *P2, cable 8, P2, K1, sl 5 sts on to cn and hold at back of work, (K2 tog, K1, K2 tog, K1)B, then (K2 tog, K3)D from cn, K1, P2, cable 8, P2, K1, sl 5 sts on to cn and hold at front of work, (K2 tog, K1, K2 tog, K1)C, then (K2 tog, K3)E from cn, K1; rep from * once more, P2, cable 8, P2.
**7th row** *P2, K8, P2, K1, K4B, K4D, K1, P2, K8, P2, K1, K4C, K4E, K1; rep from * once more, P2, K8, P2.
**9th row** As 7th row.
**11th row** *P2, cable 8, P2, K1, sl next 4 sts on to cn and

hold at front of work, K4D, then K4B from cn, K1, P2, cable 8, P2, K1, sl next 4 sts on to cn and hold at front of work, K4E, then K4C from cn, K1; rep from * once more, P2, cable 8, P2.
**13th row** *P2, K8, P2, K1, K4D, K4B, K1, P2, K8, P2, K1, K4E, K4C, K1; rep from * once more, P2, K8, P2.
**15th row** As 13th row.
**17th row** *P2, cable 8, P2, K1, sl next 4 sts on to cn and hold at front of work, (K1, make 1, K1, make 1, K2)D, then (K1, make 1, K3)D from cn, K1, P2, cable 8, P2, K1, sl next 4 sts on to cn and hold at front of work, (K1, make 1, K1, make 1, K2)E, then (K3, K into front and back of next st)E from cn, K1; rep from * once more, P2, cable 8, P2.
**19th row** *P2, K8, P2, K1, K11D, K1, P2, K8, P2, K1, K11E, K1; rep from * once more, P2, K8, P2.
**21st row** As 19th row.
**23rd row** *P2, cable 8, P2, K1, K5D, K1N, K5D, K1, P2, cable 8, P2, K1, K5E, K1L, K5E, K1; rep from * once more, P2, cable 8, P2.
**24th row** *K2, P8, K2, P1, P4E, P3L, P4E, P1, K2, P8, K2, P1, P4D, P3N, P4D, P1; rep from * once more, K2, P8, K2.
**25th row** *P2, K8, P2, K1, K3D, K5N, K3D, K1, P2, K8, P2, K1, K3E, K5L, K3E, K1; rep from * once more, P2, K8, P2.
**26th row** *K2, P8, K2, P1, P2E, P7L, P2E, P1, K2, P8, K2, P1, P2D, P7N, P2D, P1; rep from * once more, K2, P8, K2.
**27th row** As 25th row.
**28th row** As 24th row.
**29th row** As 23rd row.
**30th row** *K2, P8, K2, P1, P11E, P1, K2, P8, K2, P1, P11D, P1; rep from * once more, K2, P8, K2.
**31st row** As 19th row.
**32nd and every alt row** As 2nd row.
**33rd row** As 19th row.
**35th row** *P2, cable 8, P2, K1, K11D, K1, P2, cable 8, P2, K1, K11E, K1; rep from * once more, P2, K8, P2.
**37th row** As 19th row.
**39th row** As 19th row.
**40th row** As 2nd row.
**41st—76th rows** Rep 5th—40th rows using D instead of B, E instead of C, G instead of D, F instead of E, M instead of N and C instead of L.
**77th—112th rows** Rep 5th—40th rows using G instead of B, F instead of C, B instead of D, C instead of E, J instead of N, and H instead of L.
The 5th—112th rows form the patt rep.
Cont in patt until left front measures 45cm (17¾in) from cast-on edge, ending with a ws row.
**Shape armhole**
Keeping patt correct, cast off 33 sts at beg of next row. 79 sts.
**Shape neck**
Dec 1 st at beg of next, then every foll 3rd and 2nd row alternately until 47 sts rem.
Now work straight until front measures 22cm (8¾in) from beg of armhole shaping.
Cast off.

## RIGHT FRONT
Work as given for left front of cardigan, reversing all shapings.

## BACK

Using 2¾mm (US2) needles and yarn A, cast on 114 sts. Work 10cm (4in) in K2 tbl, P2 rib as given for left front.

**Next row** (rs) Rib 8, (rib twice into next st) to last 8 sts, rib 8. 212 sts.

Change to 3¼mm (US3) needles.

P 1 row.

Now work in long and short cable patt as for left front, placing patt within moss st borders as foll:

**1st row** (rs) (K1, P1) 25 times, work 1st row of cable patt, (P1, K1) 25 times.

**2nd row** (K1, P1) 25 times, work 2nd row of cable patt, (P1, K1) 25 times.

These 2 rows set position of cable patt and moss st borders.

Cont as set until back matches fronts to armhole, ending with a ws row.

**Shape armholes**

Cast off 18 sts at beg of next 2 rows. 176 sts.

Now work straight until back matches fronts to cast-off edge. Cast off.

## SLEEVES

Using 2¾mm (US2) needles and yarn A, cast on 62 sts. Work 10cm (4in) in K2 tbl, P2 rib as given for left front.

**Next row** (rs) Rib 1, (rib twice into next st, rib 1) to last st, rib 1. 92 sts.

Change to 3¼mm (US3) needles.

P 1 row.

Now work in cable patt as given for left front, but working only one rep and placing patt within moss st borders as foll:

**1st row** (rs) (K1, P1) 7 times, K1, P2, K8, P2, K1, K11B, K1, P2, K8, P2, K1, K11C, K1, P2, K8, P2, (K1, P1) 7 times, K1.

**2nd row** (K1, P1) 7 times, K1, work 2nd row of cable patt, (K1, P1) 7 times, K1.

These 2 rows set position of cable patt and moss st borders.

Cont as set *at the same time* inc 1 st at each end of next and every foll 5th row until there are 138 sts.

Now work straight until sleeve measures 50cm (19¾in) from cast-on edge.

Cast off.

## TO MAKE UP

Join shoulder seams.

**Front band**

Using 2¾mm (US2) needles and yarn A, cast on 11 sts. Work in K1 tbl, P1 rib until band when slightly stretched fits up left front edge, around back neck and down right front edge to beg of neck shaping.

Pin band to neck edge and mark the position of 8 buttons, one 2cm (¾in) from cast-on edge, one at beg of neck shaping, and the rest spaced evenly between.

Now cont front band until band when slightly stretched fits down right front opening, making buttonholes to correspond with button markers as foll:

**1st buttonhole row** (rs) Rib 4, cast off 3 sts, rib to end.

**2nd buttonhole row** Rib to end, casting on 3 sts over those cast off in previous row.

Cast off in rib.

Set sleeves in flat matching centre of cast-off edge to shoulder seams, and sewing last few rows of sleeve to cast-off sts at underarm.

Join side and sleeve seams.

Join on front band.

Sew on buttons.

*On the back of Long and Short Cables I've simply worked the cable panel up the centre with moss stitch on either side.*

# Cable Grape

Embossed stucco work on ceilings and fireplace surrounds was the inspiration for this piece. But, as always, I could not resist putting in some colour, though I tried to keep it soft. It would be nice to work this jacket in a collection of completely natural tones, and this would give a more realistic impression of plaster moulding.

## SIZE
**To fit** one size only up to 101cm (40in)
**Actual width measurement** 117cm (46in)
**Length to shoulder** 66cm (26in)
**Sleeve seam** 52cm (20½in)

## MATERIALS
650g (25oz) Rowan Double Knitting Wool in oatmeal 614 (A)
50g (2oz) each in pewter 88 (B), loden 89 (D), khaki 616 (E) and strawberry mousse 92 (F)
25g (1oz) in clover 602 (G)
25g (1oz) Rowan Fine Fleck Tweed in brick 412 (H)
50g (2oz) Rowan Botany Wool each in aubergine 118 (C), rose 637 (J) and mauve 121 (L)
**Equivalent yarn** double knitting
1 pair each 3mm (US2) and 3¼mm (US3) needles
3mm (US2) and 3¼mm (US3) circular needles
Cable needle
11 buttons

*NOTE: A yarn kit is available for this design. See page 143 for details.*

## TENSION
27 rows and 40 sts to 10cm (4in) over moss st on 3¼mm (US3) needles.

## SPECIAL ABBREVIATIONS
*make bobble* – (on rs rows) (K1, P1, K1, P1, K1) into next st, turn, K5, turn, P5, turn, K5, turn, P5, turn, K5, turn, P5 tog (on ws rows read K for P and P for K throughout)
*FC (front cross)* – sl 2 sts on to cable needle and hold at front of work, P1, then K2 from cable needle
*BC (back cross)* – sl 1 st on to cable needle and hold at back of work, K2, then P1 from cable needle

## BLACKBERRY STITCH
**1st row** (ws) *P3 tog, (K1, P1, K1) into next st; rep from * to end.
**2nd row** P to end.
**3rd row** *(K1, P1, K1) into next st, P3 tog; rep from * to end.
**4th row** P to end.
Rep 1st–4th rows.

## BACK
Using 3mm (US2) needles and yarn A, cast on 182 sts.
Work 10cm (4in) in K1 tbl, P1 rib.
Change to 3¼mm (US3) needles and work in colour and cable patt from chart, beg with a ws row.
Work in st st unless otherwise indicated and use separate lengths of yarn for each colour area, twisting yarns tog at colour joins to avoid holes; work 116 rows.

### Shape armholes
Dec 1 st at each end of every row until 142 sts rem.
Now work straight until back measures 23cm (9in) from beg of armhole shaping, ending with a ws row.
Cast off.

## RIGHT FRONT
Using 3mm (US2) needles and yarn A, cast on 87 sts.
Work 10cm (4in) in K1 tbl, P1 rib.
Change to 3¼mm (US3) needles and work in colour and cable patt from chart, beg with a ws row, until right front matches back to armhole, ending with a rs row.
### Shape armhole
Dec 1 st at armhole edge on every row until 67 sts rem. Work straight until right front measures 10 rows less than back to cast-off row, ending with a ws row.
### Shape neck
Cast off 9 sts at beg of next row and 7 sts at beg of foll 4 alt rows. 30 sts. Work 1 row. Cast off.

## LEFT FRONT
Work as given for right front, reversing shapings.

## SLEEVES
Using 3mm (US2) needles and yarn A, cast on 60 sts.
Work 13cm (5in) in K1 tbl, P1 rib.
**Next row** Rib 10, (rib twice in next st, rib 9) to end. 65 sts.
Change to 3¼mm (US3) needles and work 117 rows in colour and cable patt from chart, beg with a ws row, *at the same time* inc 1 st at each end of next and every foll 4th row, working the extra sts in moss st, until there are 133 sts (when 117 chart rows are completed work in moss st only).
Now work straight until sleeve measures 52cm (20½in) from cast-on edge.
### Shape top
Dec 1 st at each end of every row until 93 sts rem.
Cast off.

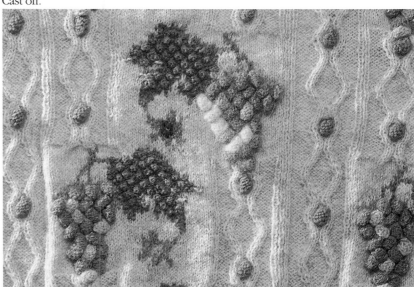

☐ = K on rs rows,
      P on ws rows in A
      unless otherwise
      indicated

☑ = P on rs rows,
      K on ws rows in A

⊞ = B      ◪ = G

◪ = C      ⊠ = H

◉ = D      ⊟ = J

♈ = E      ◺ = L

Ⅱ = F      ◿ = P1 tbl

◻ = make bobble in
      colour shown

▨ = front cross

▧ = back cross

## OUTER COLLAR

Join shoulder seams.
Using 3¼mm (US3) needles and yarn A, cast on 23 sts.
Work in colour and cable patt from chart, beg with a
ws row and working between collar markers, until
work is long enough to fit neck edge, ending with an
11th, 37th or 63rd patt row.
Cast off.

## INNER COLLAR

With rs of outer collar facing, using 3¼mm (US3)
circular needle and yarn A, K up 152 sts along one
row-ends edge. Work in rows.
Work in K4 tbl, P4 rib until inner collar measures
same as width of outer collar.
Cast off in rib.

## COLLAR EDGING

With rs of outer collar facing, using 3mm (US2)
needles and yarn A, K up 176 sts along opposite
row-ends edge.
Work 6 rows in K1, P1 rib.
Cast off in rib.

## TO MAKE UP

With ws of jacket facing, join on cast-off edge of inner
collar to neck edge.
Fold outer collar over on to rs and sew to neck edge
along join between collar and collar edging, leaving
edging free.
**Button band**
Using 3mm (US2) needles and yarn A, cast on 11 sts.
Work in K1 tbl, P1 rib until band when slightly
stretched fits up left front to collar fold. Cast off.
Join button band to left front and collar edge (closing
edges of collar at the same time).
Mark positions of 11 buttons, one 1cm (½in) from
cast-on edge, one 1cm (½in) from cast-off edge and
the rest spaced evenly between.
**Buttonhole band**
Work as given for button band, making buttonholes
opposite button markers as foll:
**1st row** Rib 4, cast off 3 sts, rib to end.
**2nd row** Rib to end, casting on 3 sts over those cast off
in previous row.
Sew on buttonhole band. Join side and sleeve seams.
Set in sleeves. Sew on buttons.

rep 1st – 78th rows

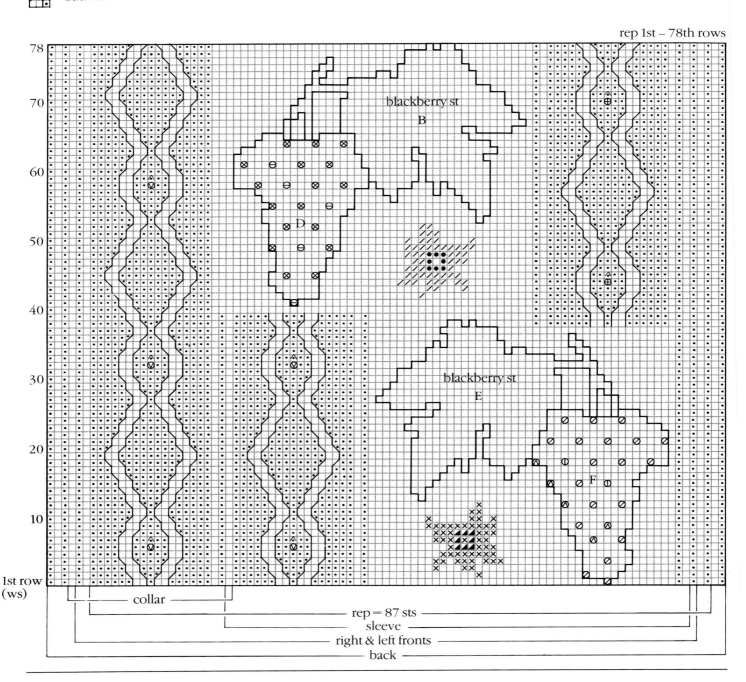

# *Aran Blouse*

This is an exercise in restraint! Designs don't have to be complicated to be effective. Here I've allowed myself one colour only for the body, which is worked in five different cables and blackberry stitch. But then I broke the rule and used *nine* different colours just in the collar and cuffs.

### SIZE
**To fit** 91cm (36in) bust
**Actual width measurement** 98cm (38½in)
**Length to shoulder** 68.5cm (27in)
**Sleeve seam** 43cm (17in)

### MATERIALS
550g (20oz) four-ply wool in main colour (A)
Oddments in each of 9 contrast colours
    (B,C,D,E,F,G,H,J,L)
1 pair each 2¼mm (US1), 3mm (US2) and 3¼mm
    (US3) needles
2¼mm (US1) circular needle
Cable needle

### TENSION
34 sts and 37 rows to 10cm (4in) over Aran patt on 3¼mm (US3) needles.

### SPECIAL ABBREVIATIONS
*wyif* – with yarn in front
*3 from 1* – (K1, P1, K1) into next st
*make bobble* – (K1, P1, K1, P1, K1) into next st, turn, K5, turn, P5, turn, K5, turn, P5 tog
*cable 6* – sl next 3 sts on to cable needle and hold at front of work, K3, then K3 from cable needle
*Left twist* – sl next 4 sts on to cable needle and hold at front of work, K3, then K4 from cable needle
*Right twist* – sl next 3 sts on to cable needle and hold at back of work, K4, then K3 from cable needle
*SBC (single back cross)* – sl 1 st on to cable needle and hold at back of work, K1, then P1 from cable needle
*SFC (single front cross)* – sl 1 st on to cable needle and hold at front of work, P1, then K1 from cable needle

### BACK
Using 2¼mm (US1) needles and yarn A, cast on 160 sts.
Work 8cm (3in) in K1 tbl, P1 rib.
Change to 3¼mm (US3) needles and beg Aran patt as foll:
**1st row** (ws) P9, *(K4, P4, K4) twice*, work 1st row of cable chart, rep from * to *, P9.
**2nd row** K9, *(P4, K4, P4) twice*, work 2nd row of cable chart, rep from * to *, K9.
**3rd row** P9, *(K4, P1, sl 2 wyif, P1, K4) twice*, work 3rd row of cable chart, rep from * to *, P9.
**4th row** K9, *(P2, sl next 3 sts on to cable needle and hold at back of work, K1, then P1, K1, P1 from cable needle, sl next st on to cable needle and hold at front of work, K1, P1, K1, then K1 from cable needle, P2) twice*, work 4th row of cable chart, rep from * to *, K9.
**5th, 7th and 9th rows** P9, *(K2, P1, K1, P1, K1, P1, K1, P2, K2) twice*, work equivalent rows from cable chart, rep from * to *, P9.
**6th, 8th and 10th rows** K9, *(P2, K1, P1, K1, P1, K1, P1, K2, P2) twice*, work equivalent rows from cable chart, rep from * to *, K9.
**11th row** P9, *(K2, sl 1 wyif, K1, P1, K1, P1, K1, P1, sl 1 wyif, K2) twice, work 11th row of cable chart, rep from * to *, P9.
**12th row** K9, *(P2, sl next st on to cable needle and hold at front of work, P2, K1, then K1 from cable needle, sl next 3 sts on to cable needle and hold at back of work, K1, then K1, P2 from cable needle, P2) twice*, work 12th row of cable chart, rep from * to *, K9.
**13th–16th rows** Rep 1st–2nd rows twice, but working 13th–16th rows of cable chart, instead of 1st–2nd rows.
These 16 rows form Aran patt.
Cont in Aran patt until back measures 48cm (19in) from cast-on edge, ending with a ws row.
**Shape armholes**
Keeping patt correct, cast off 8 sts at beg of next 2 rows. 144 sts.
Now dec 1 st at each end of next and every foll alt row until 120 sts rem.**
Now work straight until back measures 20.5cm (8in) from beg of armhole shaping, ending with a ws row.
**Shape shoulders**
Cast off 12 sts at beg of next 6 rows.
Cast off rem 48 sts.

### FRONT
Work as given for back to **
Now work straight until front measures 12 rows less than back to shoulder shaping, ending with a ws row.
**Divide for neck**
**Next row** Patt 48 sts, turn, leaving rem sts on a spare needle and cont on these sts only for first side of neck. (Cast off 2 sts at beg of next row, then dec 1 st at neck edge on foll row) 4 times. 36 sts.
Work straight until front matches back to shoulder, ending at armhole edge.
**Shape shoulder**
Cast off 12 sts at beg of next and foll alt row. 12 sts.
Work 1 row.
Cast off.
With rs of work facing, return to sts on spare needle, rejoin yarn to next st, cast off 24 sts, patt to end. 48 sts.
Complete second side of neck to match first reversing shapings.

1st row (ws)

□ = K on rs rows, P on ws rows
⊡ = P on rs rows, K on ws rows
⧆ = 3 from 1
⊞⊞ = P3 tog
◘ = make bobble

 = left twist

 = right twist

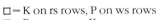 = cable 6

⊡ = SBC

⊡ = SFC

rep 1st – 16th rows

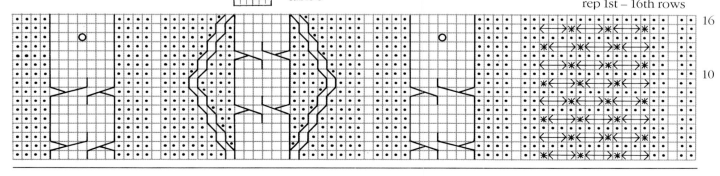

16

10

## SLEEVES

Using 3¼mm (US3) needles and yarn A, cast on 126 sts.

Work in Aran patt as foll:

**1st row** (ws) P16, work 1st row of cable chart, P16.

**2nd row** K16, work 2nd row of cable chart, K16.

These 2 rows set position of cable chart with st st panels at either side.

Cont as set until sleeve measures 43cm (17in) from cast-on edge, ending with a ws row.

### Shape top

Keeping patt correct, cast off 4 sts at beg of next 6 rows, 3 sts at beg of foll 4 rows, then dec 1 st at each end of every row until 84 sts rem.

Now dec 1 st at each end of every alt row until 76 sts rem, then at each end of every foll 3rd row until 52 sts rem on needle.

Now cast off 8 sts at beg of next 4 rows.

Cast off rem 20 sts.

## COLLAR

Using 3mm (US2) needles and yarn B, cast on 30 sts.

K 1 row.

Now work in striped blackberry st, using 2¼mm (US1) needles on ws rows and 3mm (US2) needles on rs rows, as foll:

**1st row** (ws) With yarn C, P1, (P3 tog, 3 from 1) to last st, P1.

**2nd row** With yarn C, P to end.

**3rd row** With yarn D, P1, (3 from 1, P3 tog) to last st, P1.

**4th row** With yarn D, P to end.

These 4 rows form blackberry st patt.

Cont in patt, working 2 row stripe sequence in *E,F,G,C,H,J,L,E,B,C,D**; rep from * to ** twice more.

Now work 2 rows in E, 2 rows in F, 2 rows in G.

76 rows in all have been worked, and this point marks centre back.

Now beg to reverse stripe sequence.

Work 2 rows in F, 2 rows in E. Now rep from ** to * 3 times.

Work 2 rows in D, 2 rows in C.

K 1 row in B.

Cast off in B.

## CUFFS (make 2)

Using 3mm (US2) needles and yarn B, cast on 66 sts.

K 1 row. Work 20 rows in blackberry st as for collar, working 2 row stripe sequence in C,D,E,F,G,C,H,J,L,E.

P 1 row in B. Cast off in B.

## TO MAKE UP

Join shoulder seams.

Join on collar to neck edge, matching cast-off and cast-on edges to each side of central cable at centre front.

### Collar edging

With rs of work facing, using 2¼mm (US1) circular needle and yarn A, beg at centre front, K up 30 sts along short end of collar, 80 sts across back edge and 30 sts along short end. 140 sts.

P 1 row.

**Next row** (K twice into every st) to end. 280 sts.

Work 5 rows in st st, ending with a P row.

**Next row** *K3A, 1E; rep from * to end.

**Next row** Using E, *3 from 1, P3 tog; rep from * to end.

**Next row** *K1A, P3E; rep from * to end.

**Next row** Using A, *P3 tog, 3 from 1; rep from * to end.

Using A, cast off loosely.

Join on cuffs to sleeve ends.

Join side, sleeve and cuff seams. Set in sleeves.

Overlap collar frills and sew down to neck edge.

*The collar on the Aran Blouse is worked in a striped version of blackberry stitch. I love this deep, rich rowanberry red.*

# *Fruits*

This is a version of the Cable Grape design. I've always liked Elizabethan crewel work, and the way it uses textured stitches to fill in floral motifs. Here I've used bobbles for the bunches of grapes, moss stitch for the vine leaves and blackberry stitch for the quinces.

## SIZE
**To fit** one size up to 101cm (40in)
**Actual width measurement** 108.5cm (42¾in)
**Length to shoulder** 71cm (28in)
**Sleeve seam** 50.5cm (20in) (with cuff unfolded)

## MATERIALS
400g (15oz) four-ply wool in main colour (A)
50g (2oz) in one contrast colour (B)

25g (1oz) in each of 17 contrast colours
   (C,D,E,F,G,H,J,L,M,N,Q,R,S,T,U,V,W)
1 pair each 3mm (US2) and 3¼mm (US3) needles
1 2.50mm (USC) crochet hook

## TENSION
28 sts and 34 rows to 10cm (4in) over st st on 3¼mm
(US3) needles.

## SPECIAL INSTRUCTIONS
**Blackberry stitch**
**1st row** (ws) *P3 tog, (K1, P1, K1) into next st; rep
from * to end.
**2nd row** P to end.
**3rd row** *(K1, P1, K1) into next st, P3 tog; rep from * to
end.
**4th row** P to end.
Rep these 4 rows.

□ = A
⊠ = D
◪ = C
◢ = L
◣ = Q
⊠ = M
⊡ = R
◸ = T
◢ = U
⊡ = V
⊞ = W
■ = make bobble in B
⊡ = make bobble in C

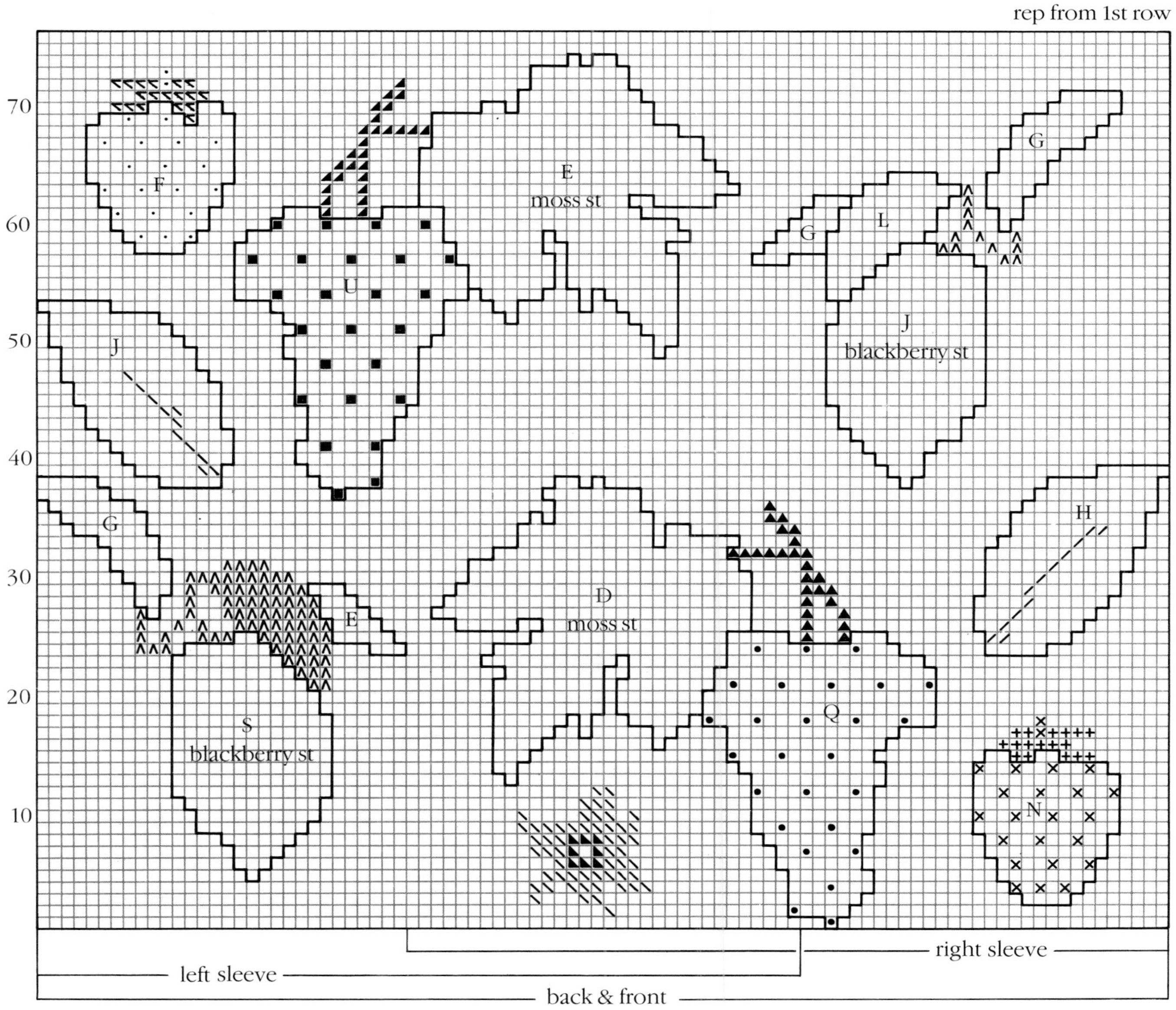

rep from 1st row

## Moss stitch

Worked over an even number of sts.
**1st row** (K1, P1) to end.
**2nd row** (P1, K1) to end.
Rep these 2 rows.
Worked over an odd number of sts.
**All rows** K1, (P1, K1) to end.

**To make bobbles** (on rs rows)
Using yarn specified, (K1, P1, K1, P1, K1) into next st, turn, K5, turn, P5, turn, K5, turn, P5 tog.
On ws rows read K for P, and P for K.

## BACK

Using 3mm (US2) needles and yarn A, cast on 152 sts.
Work 18cm (7in) in K1, P1 rib.
Change to 3¼mm (US3) needles and beg colour patt from chart 1, working in st st unless otherwise indicated and using separate lengths of yarn for each colour area, twisting yarns between colours to avoid holes, as foll:
**1st row** (rs) K30A, patt 1st row of chart, K30A.
**2nd row** P30A, patt 2nd row of chart, P30A.
These 2 rows set the position of the chart. Cont as set until back measures 46cm (18in) from cast-on edge, ending with a ws row.
**Shape armholes**
Keeping patt correct, cast off 8 sts at beg of next 2 rows. 136 sts.**
Now work straight until back measures 25cm (10in) from beg of armhole shaping, ending with a ws row.
**Shape shoulders**
Cast off 14 sts at beg of next 4 rows, then 15 sts at beg of foll 2 rows. 50 sts. Cast off.

## FRONT

Work as given for back to **.
Now work straight until front measures 18cm (7in) from beg of armhole shaping, ending with a ws row.
**Divide for neck**
**Next row** Patt 54 sts, turn, leaving rem sts on a spare needle and cont on these sts only for first side of neck.
Dec 1 st at neck edge on every row until 43 sts rem.
Now work straight until front measures same as back to shoulder, ending at armhole edge.
**Shape shoulder**
Cast off 14 sts at beg of next and foll alt row. 15 sts.
Work 1 row. Cast off.
With rs of work facing, return to sts on spare needle, rejoin yarn, cast off centre 28 sts, patt to end.
Complete second side of neck to match first side.

## LEFT SLEEVE

Using 3mm (US2) needles and yarn A, cast on 64 sts.
Work 13cm (5in) in K1, P1 rib.
**Next row** K1, P1, (K into front and back of next st, P1) to last 2 sts, K1, P1. 94 sts.
Change to 3¼mm (US3) needles and beg colour patt from chart, working between left sleeve markers, as foll:
**1st row** (rs) K16A, patt 1st row of chart, K16A.
**2nd row** P16A, patt 2nd row of chart, P16A.
These 2 rows set the position of chart patt.
Cont as set (do not work parts of motifs), *at the same time* inc 1 st at each end of next and every foll 3rd row until there are 140 sts.
Now work straight until sleeve measures 53.5cm (21in) from cast-on edge, ending with a ws row.
Cast off.

## RIGHT SLEEVE

Work as given for left sleeve, but work between right sleeve chart markers.

## COLLAR

Using 3mm (US2) needles and yarn A, cast on 148 sts.
Work in basketweave st as foll:
**1st row** (rs) K4, (P4, K4) to end.
**2nd row** P4, (K4, P4) to end.
**3rd–4th rows** As 1st–2nd rows.
**5th row** As 2nd row.
**6th row** As 1st row.
**7th–8th rows** As 5th–6th rows.
These 8 rows form the patt rep.
Cont in basketweave st until collar measures 8cm (3in).
Now work 6 rows in K1, P1 rib.
Cast off in rib.

## TO MAKE UP

Join shoulder seams.
Join on collar, matching the centre of the cast-on edge to centre back neck, and both edges at the centre front.
**Crochet collar edging**
Using 2.50 (USC) crochet hook and yarn A, beg at centre front, work shell edging around collar as foll: 2 double crochet, *(2 double crochet, 1 chain, 2 double crochet) all into next st, 2 double crochet; rep from * to end.
Set sleeves in flat, sewing final 3cm (1¼in) to cast-off sts at underarm.
Join side and sleeve seams.

*(Opposite) You usually see fruits in gaudy tropical colours, but I wanted darker, quieter tones. This colourway is in wool, but if you replace it with mercerised cotton, as right, the textured stitches are much more pronounced.*

# *Harlequin*

I've always loved colour on colour, ever since I was introduced to the painter Josef Albers' book in the Victoria and Albert Museum library. This is an incredibly ingenious catalogue of colour, arranged so that you can see vividly the way colours affect each other. The mercerised cotton yarn used in this cardigan makes the brilliant hues especially fresh and intense.

## SIZES
**To fit** 76[86,96]cm (30[34,38]in) bust
**Actual width measurement** 79[92.5,106]cm (31¼[36½,41½]in)
**Length to shoulder** 69cm (27in)
**Sleeve seam** 51cm (20in)

## MATERIALS
150[200,250]g (6[8,9]oz) Rowan Cabled Mercerised Cotton in black 319 (A)
50g (2oz) each in puce 315 (B), royal 309 (C), terracotta 314 (E), chrome 320 (G), scarlet 321 (L) delft 307 (M), cadmium 304 (N) and coral 322 (R)
50g (2oz) each Rowan Sea Breeze Soft Cotton in baize 540 (D), mermaid 547 (F), burnt orange 550 (H) and purple 543 (J)
50g (2oz) Rowan Fine Cotton Chenille in cyclamen 385 (Q)
**Equivalent yarn** four-ply
1 pair each 3mm (US2) and 3¼mm (US3) needles
9 buttons

*NOTE: A yarn kit is available for this design. See page 143 for details.*

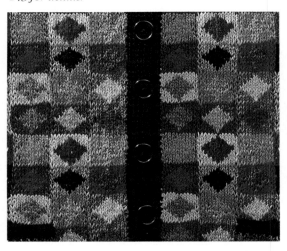

## TENSION
32 sts and 41 rows to 10cm (4in) over patt on 3¼mm (US3) needles.

## BACK
Using 3mm (US2) needles and yarn A, cast on 132[154,176] sts.
Work 5cm (2in) in K1 tbl, P1 rib.
Change to 3¼mm (US3) needles and beg colour patt from chart, working in st st throughout and rep 1st–44th rows, using separate lengths of yarn for each colour area and twisting yarns tog at colour joins to avoid holes.
Work 76 rows straight, ending with a ws row.
**Shape sides**
Dec 1 st at each end of next and every foll 9th row until 122[144,166] sts rem.
Now work straight until back measures 49cm (19¼in), ending with a ws row.
**Shape armholes**
Keeping patt correct, cast off 7 sts at beg of next 2 rows. 108[130,152] sts.
Then dec 1 st at each end of next and every foll alt row until 104[126,148] sts rem.
Now work straight until back measures 20.5cm (8in) from beg of armhole shaping, ending with a ws row.
**Shape shoulders**
Cast off 10[13,16] sts at beg of next 2 rows, and 10[14,18] sts at beg of foll 4 rows.
Cast off rem 44 sts.

## POCKET LININGS (make 2)
Using 3¼mm (US3) needles and yarn A, cast on 35 sts.
Work 48 rows in st st, ending with a P row.
Leave these sts on a spare needle.

## RIGHT FRONT
Using 3mm (US2) needles and yarn A, cast on 66[77,88] sts.
Work in 5cm (2in) in K1 tbl, P1 rib.
Change to 3¼mm (US3) needles and beg colour patt from chart, work 52 rows, thus ending with a ws row.

1st size front, 2nd size back: end rs rows, beg ws rows

2nd size front:
end rs rows, beg ws rows

sleeves:
end rs rows, beg ws rows

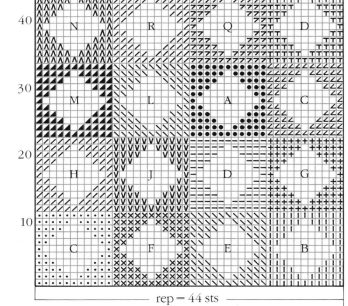

rep = 44 sts

beg all rs rows, end all ws rows

◨ = A
⊠ = B
◩ = C
◪ = D
⊡ = E
⊞ = F
▽ = G
⊟ = H
⊞ = J
◩ = L
◉ = M
⊿ = N
◪ = Q
⊤ = R

**Place pocket**
**Next row** Patt 16[22,27] sts, sl next 35 sts on to a spare needle, patt across 35 sts left on spare needle for pocket lining, patt 15[20,26].
Cont in patt, work straight until 76 rows in all have been worked from chart, ending with a ws row.
**Shape sides**
Dec 1 st at side edge on next and every foll 9th row until 61[72,83] sts rem.
Now work straight until right front matches back to armhole, ending at side edge.
**Shape armhole and front neck**
**Next row** Cast off 7 sts, patt to last 2 sts, P2 tog. 53[64,75] sts.
**Next row** Patt to end.
Now dec 1 st at armhole edge on next and foll alt row, *at the same time* dec 1 st at neck edge on every 3rd row from previous dec until 30[41,52] sts rem. Cont without shaping until front matches back to shoulder, ending at armhole edge.
**Shape shoulder**
Cast off 10[13,16] sts at beg of next row and 10[14,18] sts at beg of foll alt row.
Work 1 row. Cast off rem 10[14,18] sts.

## LEFT FRONT
Work as right front reversing pocket and shapings.

## SLEEVES
Using 3mm (US2) needles and yarn A, cast on 66 sts.
Work 16cm (6¼in) in K1 tbl, P1 rib.
**Next row** (ws) (Rib twice into next st, rib 1) to end. 99 sts.
Change to 3¼mm (US3) needles and beg colour patt from chart. Work straight until sleeve measures 51cm (20in) from cast-on edge, ending with a ws row.
**Shape top**
Cast off 7 sts at beg of next 2 rows and 2 sts at beg of foll 4 rows.
Dec 1 st at each end of next and every foll alt row until 67 sts rem, then at each end of every row until 59 sts rem. Now dec 1 st at each end of every foll 3rd row until 33 sts rem. Cast off 8 sts at beg of next 2 rows. Cast off rem 17 sts.

## POCKET TOPS
Using 3mm (US2) needles and yarn A, work 6 rows in K1 tbl, P1 rib across 35 sts left on spare needle for pocket top. Cast off in rib.

## TO MAKE UP
Join shoulder seams.
**Front bands**
Using 3mm (US2) needles and yarn A, cast on 11 sts.
Work in K1 tbl, P1 rib until band when slightly stretched fits up left front edge to beg of neck shaping. Pin band in position along left front edge and mark position of 9 buttons, one at beg of neck shaping, one 2cm (¾in) from cast-on edge and the rest spaced evenly between.
Cont in rib until band when slightly stretched, fits up left front neck around back neck, down right front neck and right front, *at the same time* make buttonholes opposite button markers as foll:
**1st buttonhole row** Rib 4, cast off 3 sts, rib to end.
**2nd buttonhole row** Rib to end, casting on 3 sts over those cast off in previous row.
Cast off in rib.
Join on front band. Join side and sleeve seams. Set in sleeves. Catch down pocket linings on ws and pocket top edges on rs. Sew on buttons.

*It's interesting to see the Harlequin cardigan styled in two quite different ways: here in a jaunty fashion and, on the previous page, in a more romantic mood.*

# *Art Deco*

I see this jacket worn for an elegant afternoon tea in a summer garden. The mercerised cotton yarn gives it a certain sleekness, and the long-lined shape and art deco motif, so evocative of the twenties, seem entirely appropriate.

## SIZE
**To fit** one size up to 91cm (36in) bust
**Actual width measurement** 98cm (38½in)
**Length to shoulder** 75cm (29½in)
**Sleeve seam** 40cm (15¾in)

## MATERIALS
450g (16oz) 4-ply mercerised cotton in main colour (A)
50g (2oz) in each of 12 contrast colours (B,C,D,E,F,G,H,J,L,M,N,Q)
1 pair each 3mm (US2) and 3¼mm (US3) needles
3mm (US2) circular needle
9 buttons

## TENSION
28 sts and 35 rows to 10cm (4in) over patt on 3¼mm (US3) needles.

## BACK
Using 3mm (US2) needles and yarn A, cast on 145 sts.
Work 7cm (2¾in) in K1 tbl, P1 rib.
Change to 3¼mm (US3) needles and beg colour patt from chart, working in st st throughout, using separate lengths of yarn for each colour area, and twisting yarns tog at colour joins to avoid holes.
Work 48 rows straight, ending with a ws row.

**Shape sides**
Keeping patt correct, dec 1 st at each end of next and every foll 9th row until 135 sts rem.
Now work straight until back measures 53cm (21in) from cast-on edge, ending with a ws row.
**Shape armholes**
Cast off 7 sts at beg of next 2 rows. Now dec 1 st at each end of next and every foll alt row until 113 sts rem.
Now work straight until back measures 22cm (8¾in) from beg of armhole shaping, ending with a ws row.
**Shape shoulders**
Cast off 12 sts at beg of next 6 rows. 41 sts.
Cast off.

## POCKET LININGS (make 2)
Using 3¼mm (US3) needles and yarn A, cast on 35 sts.
Work 44 rows in st st, ending with a ws row.
Leave these sts on a spare needle.

## RIGHT FRONT
Using 3mm (US2) needles and yarn A, cast on 72 sts.
Work 7cm (2¾in) in K1 tbl, P1 rib.
Change to 3¼mm (US3) needles and work 46 rows in colour patt from chart, ending with a ws row.
**Place pocket**
**Next row** Patt 19 sts, sl next 35 sts on to a spare needle for pocket edging, patt across 35 sts of pocket lining, patt 18 sts.
Patt 1 row.
**Shape side**
Dec 1 st at end of next and every foll 9th row until 67 sts rem.
Now work straight until right front matches back to armhole, ending at side edge.

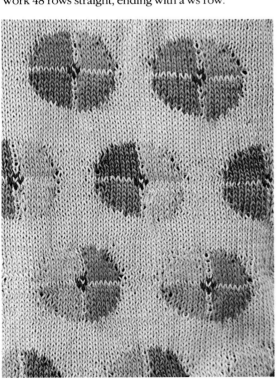 

*This simple geometrical pattern lends itself to many colourways. Seeing these two samples side by side, you'll notice how in the delphinium soft cotton version the colours appear much denser than in the mercerised cotton one where the shine on the yarn makes them seem paler.*

□ = A    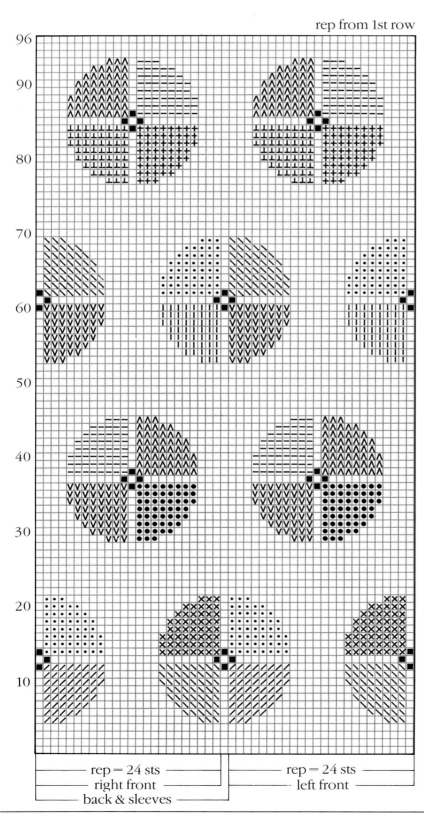 = H
▨ = B    ⊟ = J
◨ = C    Ⅱ = L
⊡ = D    ⊞ = M
⊠ = E    Ⅱ = N
⊙ = F    ■ = Q
Ⅴ = G

**Shape armhole and front neck**
**Next row** Cast off 7 sts, patt to last 2 sts, P2 tog.
Keeping patt correct, dec 1 st at armhole edge on next
and 7 foll alt rows, *at the same time* dec 1 st at neck
edge on every foll 4th row until 36 sts rem.
Now work straight until right front matches back to
shoulder, ending at armhole edge.
**Shape shoulder**
Cast off 12 sts at beg of next and foll alt row.
Work 1 row.
Cast off.

rep from 1st row

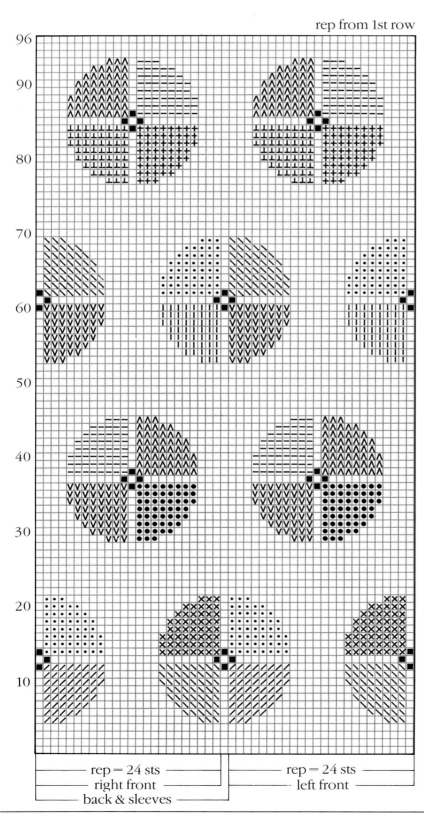

rep = 24 sts — right front
rep = 24 sts — left front
back & sleeves

## LEFT FRONT
Work as given for right front, reversing pocket placing
and all shapings.

## SLEEVES
Using 3mm (US2) needles and yarn A, cast on 64 sts.
Work 9cm (3½in) in K1 tbl, P1 rib.
**Next row** Inc 33 sts evenly across row. 97 sts.
Change to 3¼mm (US3) needles and work in chart
patt, beg at 29th row, until sleeve measures 40cm
(15¾in) from cast-on edge, ending with a ws row.
**Shape top**
Keeping patt correct, cast off 3 sts at beg of next 6 rows
and 2 sts at beg of foll 4 rows. 71 sts.
Now dec 1 st at each end of every row until 63 sts rem,
then on every foll alt row until 55 sts rem, then on
every foll 3rd row until 37 sts rem.
Cast off 6 sts at beg of next 4 rows. 13 sts.
Cast off.

## FRONT BANDS AND COLLAR
Join shoulder seams.
Using 3mm (US2) needles and yarn A, cast on 10 sts.
Work in K1 tbl, P1 rib until left front band when
slightly stretched fits up to beg of front neck shaping,
ending at inner front edge.
**Shape collar**
Now work in moss st, inc 1 st at end of next and every
foll alt row until there are 22 sts. Mark corresponding
position of length of band on right front with
coloured thread.
Work straight until collar fits to coloured marker,
ending at inner neck edge.
Cont in moss st, dec 1 st at end of next and every alt
row until 10 sts rem.
Place 9 button markers on left front band, one 1cm
(½in) from cast-on edge and one at beg of collar
shaping, and the rest spaced evenly between.
**Work right front band**
Cont in K1 tbl, P1 rib, making buttonholes to
correspond with button markers on left front band as
foll:
**1st buttonhole row** (rs) Rib 4, cast off 2 sts, rib to end.
**2nd buttonhole row** Rib to end, casting on 2 sts over
those cast off in previous row.
Cont in this way until right front band matches left
front band to cast-on edge.
Cast off in rib.

## POCKET EDGINGS
Using 3mm (US2) needles and yarn A, work in K1 tbl,
P1 rib across 35 sts left on spare needle for pocket
edgings.
Rib 6 rows.
Cast off in rib.

## TO MAKE UP
Join on collar and front bands, matching centre of
collar to centre back neck, and stretching front bands
slightly to fit between cast-on edges of fronts and beg
of front neck shaping.
Fold collar on to rs.
**Collar edging**
With rs of collar facing, using 3mm (US2) circular
needle and yarn A, K up 240 sts evenly around edge of
collar.
Place a marker on point of each 'lapel'. Work in rows.
Rib 4 rows, inc 1 st at each side of markers on every
row. 256 sts.
Cast off in rib.
Join side and sleeve seams.
Set in sleeves.
Catch down pocket tops and linings.
Join row ends of collar edging to front bands.
Sew on buttons.

# *Fans*

This design is based on a traditional American patchwork quilt made up of striped fan shapes. But rather than work it on a plain background, I chose a closely toned chequerboard. This enhances the abstract quality so that the fans become lost in strong diagonal waves.

## SIZES
### Sweater
To fit 86–91[96–101]cm (34–36[38–40]in) bust/chest
**Actual width measurements** 100[110]cm (39½[43¼]in)
**Length to shoulder** 70[75]cm (27½[29½]in)
**Sleeve seam** 57cm (22½in)
### Cardigan
**To fit** one size only up to 101cm (40in) bust/chest
**Actual width measurement** 115cm (45¼in)
**Length to shoulder** 69cm (27¼in)
**Sleeve seam** 51cm (20in)

## MATERIALS
### Sweater
300[350]g (11[13]oz) four-ply wool in main colour (A)
50g (2oz) in each of 16 contrast colours
   (B,C,D,E,F,G,H,J,L,M,N,Q,R,S,T,U)

### Cardigan
400g (15oz) four-ply wool in main colour (A)
50g (2oz) in each of 16 contrast colours
   (B,C,D,E,F,G,H,J,L,M,N,Q,R,S,T,U)
1 pair each 3mm (US2) and 3¼mm (US3) needles
Cable needle (cardigan only)
10 buttons (cardigan only)

## TENSION
28 sts and 32 rows to 10cm (4in) over patt on 3¼mm (US3) needles.

## SWEATER

### BACK
Using 3mm (US2) needles and yarn A, cast on 140[154] sts.
Work 6.5cm (2½in) in K1 tbl, P1 rib.
Change to yarn G and K 2 rows.
Change to yarn A and rib 5cm (2in).
Change to 3¼mm (US3) needles and beg colour patt from chart, working in st st throughout, using separate lengths of yarn for each colour area, and twisting yarns tog at colour joins to avoid holes.
Work straight until back measures 45[50]cm (17¾[19¾]in) from cast-on edge, ending with a ws row.
**Shape armholes**
Cast off 8[9] sts at beg of next 2 rows. 124[136] sts.**
Now work straight until back measures 25cm (9¾in) from beg of armhole shaping, ending with a ws row.
**Shape shoulders**
Cast off 12[14] sts at beg of next 6 rows. 52 sts.

### FRONT
Work as given for back to **.
Now work straight until front measures 14 rows less than back to beg of shoulder shaping, ending with a ws row.
**Divide for neck**
**Next row** Patt 44[50] sts, turn, leaving rem sts on a spare needle, and cont on these sts only for first side of neck.
Cont in patt, dec 1 st at neck edge on every row until 36[42] sts rem.
Now work straight until front matches back to shoulder, ending at armhole edge.
**Shape shoulder**
Cast off 12[14] sts at beg of next and foll alt row. 12[14] sts.
Work 1 row.
Cast off.
With rs of work facing, return to sts on spare needle, rejoin yarn to next st, cast off 36 sts, patt to end. 44[50] sts.
Complete second side of neck to match first, reversing shapings.

### SLEEVES
Using 3mm (US2) needles and yarn A, cast on 66 sts.
Work 12cm (4¾in) in K1 tbl, P1 rib.
Next row (Rib 1, rib twice into next st) to last 2 sts, rib 2. 98 sts.

⊠ = U

cardigan fronts: beg ws rows, end rs rows |          rep 1st – 56th rows

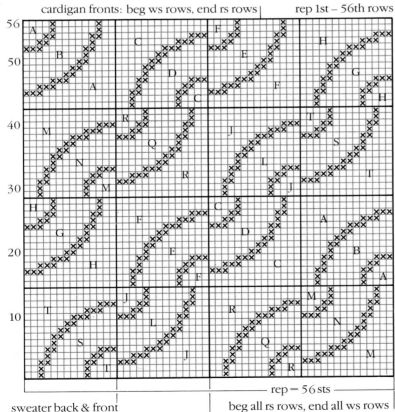

sweater back & front
2nd size/sleeves both sizes:
beg ws rows, end rs rows | beg all rs rows, end all ws rows |

rep = 56 sts

sweater back & front 1st size: beg ws rows, end rs rows

Change to 3¼mm (US3) needles and work in colour patt from chart, *at the same time* inc 1 st at each end of next and every foll 3rd row until there are 140 sts.
Now work straight until sleeve measures 60cm (23½in) from cast-on edge.
Cast off.

### COLLAR
Using 3mm (US2) needles and yarn A, cast on 132 sts.
Work 8cm (3in) in K1 tbl, P1 rib.
Cast off in rib.

### COLLAR EDGINGS
With rs of work facing, using 3mm (US2) needles and yarn A, K up 26 sts evenly along row-ends edge of collar.
Work 7 rows in K1 tbl, P1 rib.
Cast off in rib.
Make a similar edging on opposite edge of collar.

### TO MAKE UP
Join shoulder seams.
Sew on collar, matching centre of cast-on edge to centre back and collar edges to centre front, overlapping collar edgings left over right.
Set in sleeves flat, matching centre of cast-off edge to shoulder seams and joining last few rows of sleeve to cast-off sts at underarm.
Join side and sleeve seams.

## CARDIGAN

*(Opposite) The Fans pattern is arranged quite differently on the cardigan. Whereas the pattern is all over the sweater, here it runs in a panel up the centre back and sleeves, and there is a deep, cabled welt.*

*(Below) A soft clover with warm brick tones and areas picked out in angora.*

### BACK
Using 3mm (US2) needles and yarn A, cast on 160 sts.
Work 2.5cm (1in) in K1, P1 rib.
Change to 3¼mm (US3) needles and work in cable rib as foll:
**1st row** (rs) K4, (P2, K4) to end.
**2nd row** K all the P sts and P all the K sts of previous row.
**3rd–4th rows** As 1st–2nd rows.
**5th row** K4, *P2, sl next 2 sts on to cable needle and hold at front of work, K2, then K2 from cable needle, P2, K4; rep from * to end.
**6th row** As 2nd row.
These 6 rows form cable rib patt.

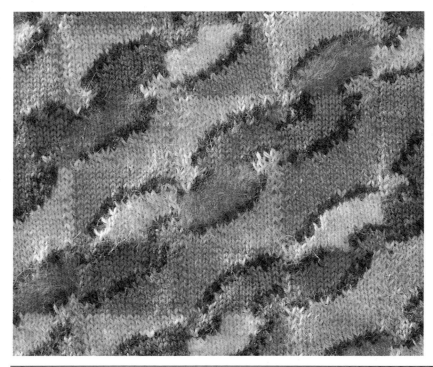

Cont in cable rib until back measures 16cm (6¼in) from cast-on edge, ending with a ws row.
Now work in colour patt from chart, working in st st throughout, using separate lengths of yarn for each colour area, and twisting yarns tog at colour joins to avoid holes, as foll:
**1st row** (rs) K24A, (patt 1st row of chart) twice, K24A.
**2nd row** P24A, (patt 2nd row of chart) twice, P24A.
These 2 rows set chart patt.
Cont as set until back measures 46cm (18in) from cast-on edge, ending with a ws row.
**Shape raglan armholes**
\*\*Dec 1 st at each end of next 3 rows.
Work 1 row.\*\*
Rep from \*\* to \*\* until 40 sts rem. Cast off.

### RIGHT FRONT
Using 3mm (US2) needles and yarn A, cast on 76 sts.
Work 2.5cm (1in) in K1, P1 rib.
Change to 3¼mm (US3) needles and work 16cm (6¼in) in cable rib as for back, ending with a ws row.
Now work in colour patt from chart working between front markers, until right front matches back to armhole, ending with a ws row.
**Shape raglan armhole and front neck**
\*\*Dec 1 st at armhole edge on next 3 rows.
Work 1 row.\*\* 73 sts.
Rep from \*\* to \*\* 3 times more. 64 sts.
Now rep from \*\* to \*\* 16 times more, *at the same time* dec 1 st at front neck on next and every foll 4th row until 2 sts rem. Work 1 row. Fasten off.

### LEFT FRONT
Work as given for right front, reversing shapings.

### SLEEVES
Using 3mm (US2) needles and yarn A, cast on 52 sts.
Work 12cm (4¾in) in K1, P1 rib.
**Next row** (Rib twice into next st, rib 1) to end. 78 sts.
Change to 3¼mm (US3) needles and work in colour patt as foll:
**1st row** (rs) K11A, patt 1st row of chart, K11A.
**2nd row** P11A, patt 2nd row of chart, P11A.
These 2 rows set position of chart patt.
Cont as set, *at the same time* inc 1 st at each end of next and every foll 3rd row until there are 140 sts, working the incs in st st in A.
Now work straight until sleeve measures 51cm (20in) from cast-on edge, ending with a ws row.
**Shape top**
\*\*Dec 1 st at each end of next 3 rows.
Work 1 row.
Dec 1 st at each end of next 4 rows.\*\*
Rep from \*\* to \*\* 9 times more. Fasten off.

### TO MAKE UP
Join raglan seams
**Front bands**
Using 3mm (US2) needles and yarn A, cast on 11 sts.
Work in K1, P1 rib until band when slightly stretched fits up left front edge to beg of neck shaping.
Pin band in position along left front edge and mark position of 10 buttons, one at beg of neck shaping, one 2cm (¾in) from cast-on edge and the rest spaced evenly between.
Now cont in rib until band when slightly stretched fits up left front neck, around back neck, down right front neck and right front, *at the same time* make buttonholes opposite button markers as foll:
**1st buttonhole row** (rs) Rib 4, cast off 3 sts, rib to end.
**2nd buttonhole row** Rib to end, casting on 3 sts over those cast off in previous row.
Cast off in rib.
Join on front bands. Join side and sleeve seams.
Sew on buttons.

# Asymmetric

It is interesting to experiment with areas of patterning. In this way you can disguise certain parts of yourself – like large shoulders or wide hips – and enhance others. Placing a strong pattern on one side of a neutral background, as here, has the optical effect of making you taller and thinner. The repeating block pattern seen in many early quilts continues over the right shoulder, so that the back is a mirror image of the front.

## SIZE
**To fit** one size only up to 96cm (38in) bust
**Actual width measurement** 101cm (40in)
**Length to shoulder** 62.5cm (24½in)
**Sleeve seam** 42cm (16½in)

## MATERIALS
400g (15oz) four-ply cotton in main colour (A)
50g (2oz) in each of 11 contrast colours (B,C,D,E,F,G,H,J,L,M,N)
1 pair each 3mm (US2) and 3¼mm (US3) needles
8 buttons

## TENSION
30 sts and 35 rows to 10cm (4in) over basketweave patt on 3¼mm (US3) needles.

## BACK
Using 3mm (US2) needles and yarn A, cast on 152 sts.
Work in K4, P4 rib as foll:
**1st row** (rs) (K4, P4) to end.
Rep this row until work measures 7cm (2¾in) from cast-on edge, ending with a ws row.
Change to 3¼mm (US3) needles and work in basketweave patt as foll:
**1st–4th rows** (P4, K4) to end.
**5th–8th rows** (K4, P4) to end.
These 8 rows form the patt rep.
Cont in basketweave patt until back measures 22cm (8¾in) from cast-on edge, ending with a 4th or 8th patt row.**
Now keeping basketweave patt correct as set, beg colour patt from chart 1, using separate lengths of yarn for each colour area and twisting yarns tog at colour joins to avoid holes, as foll:
**Next row** Work 14 sts in basketweave patt in A, (K in patt across 1st row of chart 1) twice, work 58 sts in basketweave patt in A.
**Next row** Work 58 sts in basketweave patt in A, (P in patt across 2nd row of chart 1) twice, work 14 sts in basketweave patt in A.
These 2 rows set position of chart 1 and basketweave patt.
Cont as set until back measures 36cm (14in) from cast-on edge, ending with a ws row (work chart patt in st st throughout).
## Shape armholes
Cast off 7 sts at beg of next 2 rows. 138 sts.
Now work straight until back measures 26.5cm (10½in) from beg of armhole shaping, ending with a ws row.

## Shape shoulders
Cast off 15 sts at beg of next 2 rows, and 16 sts at beg of foll 4 rows.
Cast off rem 44 sts.

## FRONT
Work as given for back to ** placing chart 1 as foll:
**Next row** Work 58 sts in basketweave patt in A, (K in patt across 1st row of chart 1) twice, work 14 sts in basketweave patt in A.
### Divide for front opening
**Next row** Work 54 sts in basketweave patt in A, turn, leaving rem sts on a spare needle, and cont on these sts only for first side of front opening.
Work straight until front matches back to armhole, ending with a ws row.
### Shape armhole
Cast off 7 sts at beg of next row. 47 sts.
Now work straight until front matches back to shoulder, ending at armhole edge.
### Shape shoulder
Cast off 15 sts at beg of next row and 16 sts at beg of foll alt row. 16 sts.
Work 1 row.
Cast off.
With rs of work facing, return to sts on spare needle, sl next 4 sts on to a safety pin and beg colour patt from chart 1 as foll:
**Next row** (rs) (K in patt across 1st row of chart 1) twice, work 14 sts in basketweave patt in A.
**Next row** Work 14 sts in basketweave patt in A, (P in patt across 2nd row of chart 1) twice.
These 2 rows set the position of chart 1 and basketweave patt.
Cont as set until front matches back to armhole, ending with a rs row.

CHART 1          rep 1st – 40th rows

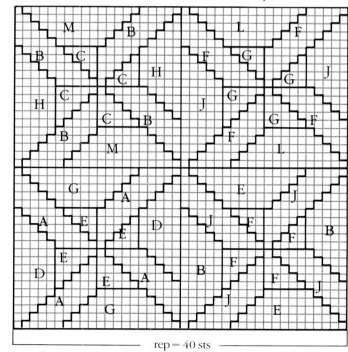

rep = 40 sts

**CHART 2**    rep 1st – 56th rows

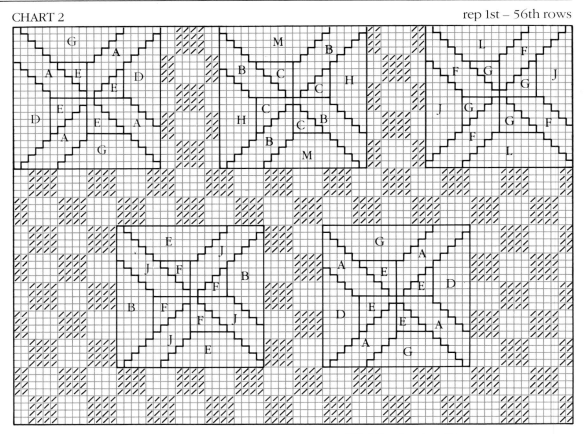

Work in A unless otherwise indicated

☐ = K on rs rows,
P on ws rows

☑ = P on rs rows,
K on ws rows

**Shape armhole**
Cast off 7 sts, patt to end. 87 sts.
Now work straight until front measures 20cm (8in) from beg of armhole shaping, ending with a ws row.
**Shape neck**
Cast off 40 sts at beg of next row. 47 sts.
Work straight until front matches back to shoulder, ending at armhole edge.
**Shape shoulder**
Cast off 15 sts at beg of next row, and 16 sts at beg of foll alt row. 16 sts.
Work 1 row.
Cast off.

**LEFT SLEEVE**
Using 3mm (US2) needles and yarn A, cast on 72 sts.
Work 10cm (4in) in K4, P4 rib as given for back of sweater.
**Next row** Inc 4 sts evenly across row. 76 sts. ***
Change to 3¼mm (US3) needles and work in basketweave patt as given for back, *at the same time* inc 1 st at each end of every foll 3rd and foll 2nd row alternately until there are 160 sts.
Work straight until 120 rows have been worked in basketweave patt.
Cast off in patt.

**RIGHT SLEEVE**
Work as given for left sleeve to ***.
Change to 3¼mm (US3) needles and beg colour patt from chart 2, placing basketweave patt and st st colour panels as shown on chart, *at the same time* inc 1 st at each end of every foll 3rd and foll 2nd row alternately until there are 160 sts, working the extra sts in basketweave patt.
Work straight until 120 rows have been worked from chart.
Cast off in patt.

**COLLAR**
Using 3mm (US2) needles and yarn A, cast on 132 sts.
Work in K4, P4 rib as foll:

**1st row** (K4, P4) to last 4 sts, K4.
**2nd row** (P4, K4) to last 4 sts, P4.
Rep these 2 rows 12 times more.
Cast off in rib.

**BUTTON BAND**
Using 3mm (US2) needles and yarn A, cast on 8 sts.
Cont in K1, P1 rib until band, when slightly stretched measures 34cm (13½in) from cast-on edge.
Cast off in rib.
Sew button band to left front, behind sts on safety pin at centre front, and ending level with right front neck shaping.
Mark position of 8 buttons, the first 3cm (1¼in) above centre front neck, and the last 2cm (¾in) below neck edge, with the rest spaced evenly between.

**BUTTONHOLE BAND**
With rs of work facing, using 3mm (US2) needles and yarn A, return to 4 sts on safety pin and front neck, rejoin yarn and work in K1, P1 rib to end.
Inc 1 st at end of next row and at same edge on 3 foll alt rows. 8 sts.
Cont in K1, P1 rib until band is same length as button band, *at the same time* make buttonholes opposite button markers as foll:
**1st buttonhole row** (rs) Rib 3, cast off 3, rib to end.
**2nd buttonhole row** Rib to end, casting on 3 sts over those cast off in previous row.
Cast off in rib.

**TO MAKE UP**
Join on buttonhole band to right front. Catch down lower shaped edge.
Join shoulder seams.
Sew on collar, positioning just over inner edge on front bands.
Set in sleeves flat, matching centre of cast-off edge to shoulder seam, and sewing last few rows of sleeve to cast-off sts at underarm.
Join side and sleeve seams.
Sew on buttons.

# Chequers

This is a scaled down version of the woven interlace pattern used in the kimono on page 68. That is an elaborate ridged variation, but here I've simply varied the colours, and it's also interesting that the smaller the rectangles are, the more embossed the pattern appears. The basketweave effect is also enhanced by using a mix of light and dark tones. The stitch is created by working turning rows – but that's not as formidable as you might think.

## SIZE

**To fit** one size only up to 101cm (40in) bust
**Actual width measurement** 112cm (44in)
**Length to shoulder** 67cm (26½in)
**Sleeve seam** 49cm (19¼in)

## MATERIALS

200g (8oz) four-ply wool in main colour (A) (used for cuffs, yolk and bands)
100g (4oz) in each of seven contrast colours (B,C,D,E,F,G,H)
1 pair each 3mm (US2) and 3¼mm (US3) needles
3mm (US2) circular needle
2.50mm (USC) crochet hook
10 buttons

## TENSION

7 rectangles measure approx 16cm (6¼in) wide by 16cm (6¼in) deep, over patt using 3¼mm (US3) needles.

## BACK

Using 3¼mm (US3) needles and yarn A, cast on 96 sts loosely and evenly.
K 1 row.
Work base row of triangles by working turning rows as foll:
**1st row** (ws) P2, turn.
**2nd row** K2.
**3rd row** P3, turn.
**4th row** K3.
**5th row** P4, do not turn.
The first triangle is completed.
Leave these 4 sts on right-hand needle and rep 1st–5th rows 23 times more so that all sts on left-hand needle are worked off and there are 24 triangles in all on right-hand needle.
Turn.
Beg first row of rectangles as foll:
**Work selvedge triangle**
**1st row** (rs) K2, turn.
**2nd row** P2.
**3rd row** K into front and back of next st, sl 1, K1, psso, turn.
**4th row** P3.
**5th row** K into front and back of next st, K1, sl 1, K1, psso.
Selvedge triangle is now completed.
Leave these 4 sts on right-hand needle.
Change to yarn B.
**Work first rectangle**
**\*\*1st row** K up 4 sts down rem side of first triangle, turn.
**2nd row** P4, turn.

**3rd row** K3, sl 1, K1, psso (using first st of next triangle), turn.
Rep 2nd–3rd rows until all sts from base triangle have been worked off.**
Rep from ** to ** using yarn A.
Cont in this way working rectangles alternately in yarn A and yarn B until 23 rectangles in all have been completed.

**Work selvedge triangle**
**1st row** Using A, K up 4 sts down rem side of last triangle.
**2nd row** P2 tog, P2, turn.
**3rd row** K3.
**4th row** P2 tog, P1, turn.
**5th row** K2.
**6th row** P2 tog.
Change to yarn C.

**Work second row of rectangles**
***1st row** P up 3 sts down side of selvedge triangle, turn. 4 sts.
**2nd row** K4.
**3rd row** P3, P2 tog (using 1 st from next rectangle), turn.
Rep 2nd–3rd rows until all sts from next rectangle have been worked off.***
Change to yarn D and rep from *** to *** picking up 4 sts from side of rectangle instead of selvedge triangle for 1st row.
Cont in this way working rectangles alternately in yarn C and yarn D until 24 rectangles in all have been completed.
Work third row of rectangles as given for first row of rectangles using yarns E and F instead of yarns A and B.
Work fourth row of rectangles as given for second row of rectangles using yarns G and H instead of yarns C and D.
These four rows of rectangles form the patt rep.
Keeping patt correct, work straight until back measures approx 57cm (22½in) from cast-on edge ending with a first row of rectangles.
Change to yarn A.
Cast off as foll:
**Next row** P up 4 sts from side of selvedge triangle, turn. 5 sts.
**Next row** K5.
**Next row** P2 tog, P2, P2 tog, turn.
**Next row** K4.
**Next row** P2 tog, P1, P2 tog, turn.
**Next row** K3.
**Next row** (P2 tog) twice, turn.
**Next row** K2.
**Next row** P3 tog.
Cont in this way until last rectangle is cast off.
Fasten off rem st.

### FRONTS (alike)
Using 3¼mm (US3) needles and yarn A, cast on 48 sts loosely and evenly.
Cont in patt as given for back but on a base row of 12 triangles instead of 24, until work matches back to end.
Cast off as for back.

### SLEEVES
Using 3¼mm (US3) needles and yarn A, cast on 80 sts loosely and evenly.
Work in patt as given for back, but working on a base row of 20 triangles instead of 24, until sleeve measures approx 34cm (13½in) from cast-on edge, ending with special cast-off method as given for back.

### BACK NECK BORDER
With rs of work facing, using 3mm (US2) circular needle and yarn A, K up 140 sts evenly along cast-off edge of back.
Work in rows.
Work 5cm (2in) in K1 tbl, P1 rib.
Cast off in rib.

### RIGHT FRONT NECK BORDER
With rs of work facing, using 3mm (US2) needles and yarn A, K up 70 sts evenly along cast-off edge of right front.
Work 2cm (¾in) in K1 tbl, P1 rib, ending with a ws row.
**Shape neck**
**Next row** Cast off 12 sts, rib to end. 58 sts.
Now dec 1 st at neck edge on next and foll 4 alt rows. 53 sts.
Work straight until front neck border matches back neck border to cast-off edge.
Cast off in rib.

### LEFT FRONT NECK BORDER
Work as given for right front border, reversing all shaping.

### CUFFS (make 2)
With rs of work facing, using 3mm (US2) needles and yarn A, K up 74 sts evenly along the cast-on edge of the sleeve.
Work in K1 tbl, P1 rib, *at the same time* dec 1 st at each end of every foll 4th row until 58 sts rem.
Cont in rib until cuff measures 15cm (6in) from K-up edge.
Cast off in rib.

### TO MAKE UP
Join shoulder seams.
Set in sleeves flat, matching centre of cast-off edge to shoulder seams.
Join side and sleeve seams.
**Welt**
With rs of work facing, using 3mm (US2) circular needle and yarn A, K up 280 sts evenly around lower edge of back and fronts.
Work in rows.
Work 5cm (2in) in K1 tbl, P1 rib.
Cast off in rib.
**Button band**
Using 3mm (US2) needles and yarn A, cast on 11 sts firmly.
Work in K1 tbl, P1 rib until band when slightly stretched fits up left front.
Cast off in rib.
Mark the positions of 10 buttons, one 1cm (½in) from cast-on edge and one 1cm (½in) from cast-off edge and the rest spaced evenly between.
**Buttonhole band**
Work as given for button band making buttonholes to correspond with button markers as foll:
**1st buttonhole row** Rib 4, cast off 3 sts, rib to end of row.
**2nd buttonhole row** Rib to end, casting on 3 sts over those cast off in previous row.
Join on button and buttonhole bands stretching them slightly to fit.
**Crochet neck edging**
Using 2.50mm (USC) crochet hook and yarn A, work picot edging as foll:
**1st row** Work in double crochet around neck edge of cardigan.
**2nd row** *1 double crochet into each of next 3 double crochet, 4 chain, slipstitch into last double crochet; rep from * around neck edge.
Fasten off.
Sew on buttons.

*(Opposite) With so many blues in it, this demure cardigan goes equally well with jeans.*

# *Kimono*

This interlaced stitch pattern lends itself to endless experimentation and I have worked a great many variations on this theme. Here each rectangle is 'piped' with striped ridges. The coat is a generous size and it really is quite a challenge to knit!

## SIZE
**To fit** one size only up to 111cm (44in) bust/chest
**Actual width measurement** 158cm (62in)
**Length to shoulder** 89cm (35in)
**Sleeve seam** 69cm (27¼in) cuff unfolded

## MATERIALS
900g (32oz) four-ply yarn in main colour (A)
75g (3oz) in each of 6 contrast colours (B,C,D,E,F,G)
50g (2oz) in each of 8 contrast colours
   (H,J,L,M,N,Q,R,S)
1 pair each 3mm (US2) and 3¼mm (US3) needles
1 each 3mm (US2) and 3¼mm (US3) circular needles

## TENSION
1 rectangle measures approx 11cm (4½in) wide by 11cm (4½in) deep, over patt on 3¼mm (US3) needles.

## BACK AND FRONTS (one piece)
Using 3¼mm (US3) circular needle and yarn A, cast on 224 sts loosely.
Work base row of triangles by working turning rows as foll:
**1st row** (ws) P2, turn.
**2nd row** K2.
**3rd row** P3, turn.
**4th row** K3
**5th row** P4, turn.
**6th row** K4.
**7th row** P5, turn.
**8th row** K5.
**9th row** P6, turn.
**10th row** K6.
**11th row** P7, turn.
**12th row** K7.
**13th row** P8, turn.
**14th row** K8.
**15th row** P9, turn.
**16th row** K9.
**17th row** P10, turn.
**18th row** K10.
**19th row** P11, turn.
**20th row** K11.
**21st row** P12, turn.
**22nd row** K12.
**23rd row** P13, turn.
**24th row** K13.
**25th row** P14, turn.
**26th row** K14.
**27th row** P15, turn.
**28th row** K15.
**29th row** P16, do not turn.
The first triangle has now been completed.
Leave these 16 sts on right-hand needle and rep 1st–29th rows 13 times more so that all sts on left-hand needle are worked off and there are 14 triangles on right-hand needle.
**Work selvedge triangle**
**1st row** (rs) K2, turn.
**2nd row** P2.
**3rd row** K into front and back of next st, sl 1, K1, psso, turn.
**4th row** P3.
**5th row** K into front and back of next st, K1, sl 1, K1, psso, turn.
**6th row** P4.
**7th row** K into front and back of next st, K2, sl 1, K1, psso, turn.
**8th row** P5.
**9th row** K into front and back of next st, K3, sl 1, K1, psso, turn.
**10th row** P6.
Cont in this way until the row 'K into front and back of next st, K12, sl 1, K1, psso, turn' has been worked.
**Next row** P15.
**Next row** K into front and back of next st, K13, sl 1, K1, psso, do not turn.
Selvedge triangle has now been completed.
Leave these 16 sts on right-hand needle.
**Work first rectangle**
**\*\*1st row** K up 16 sts along rem side of base triangle, turn.
**2nd row** P16, turn.
**3rd row** K15, sl 1, K1, psso (using 1st st of next triangle), turn.
**4th row** As 2nd row.
**5th row** As 3rd row.
**6th row** As 2nd row.
**7th–13th rows** Work in st st on these 16 sts in yarn B. Break off B.
**14th row** Using yarn A, P tog 1st st in 1st row of B and 1st st on left-hand needle, P tog 2nd st in 1st row of B and next st on left-hand needle, cont in this way across row to form 'piped cord' on rs of work, turn.
**15th row** As 3rd row
**16th row** As 2nd row.
**17th–18th rows** Rep last 2 rows.
**19th row** K(3H, 1A) to end.
**20th row** P(1A, 3H) to end.
**21st–24th rows** Rep 19th–20th rows twice.
**25th row** As 19th row.
**26th row** As 14th row reading 'H and A' for 'B'.
**27th–30th rows** As 15th–18th rows.
**31st–37th rows** As 19th–25th rows using J instead of H, and L instead of A.
**38th row** As 14th row reading 'J and L' for 'B'.
**39th–42nd rows** As 15th–18th rows.
**43rd–49th rows** As 19th–25th rows using M instead of H.
**50th row** As 14th row reading 'M and A' for 'B'.
**51st row** As 3rd row.
Rep 2nd–3rd rows until all sts from base triangle have been worked off.\*\*
One rectangle has now been completed.
Rep from \*\* to \*\* 12 times more to complete 13 rectangles in all.
**Work selvedge triangle**
**1st row** Using yarn A, K up 16 sts along rem side of base triangle.

**2nd row** P2 tog, P14, turn.
**3rd and every alt row** K to end.
**4th row** P2 tog, P13, turn.
**6th row** P2 tog, P12, turn.
Cont in this way until 1 st rem.
First row of rectangles has now been completed.
**Work second row of rectangles**
***1st row** With A, P up 15 sts along side of selvedge triangle, turn. 16 sts.
**2nd row** K16.
**3rd row** P15, P2 tog (using 1 st from next rectangle), turn.
**4th–7th rows** Rep 2nd–3rd rows twice.
****8th–14th rows** Work in st st in yarn C. Break off C.
**15th row** Using yarn A, P tog 1 st in 1st row of C and 1st st on left-hand needle, cont in this way across row to form 'piped cord' on rs of work, turn.
**16th row** As 2nd row.
**17th row** As 3rd row.
**18th–19th rows** As 16th–17th rows.****
**20th–31st rows** Rep from **** to **** using N instead of C.
**32nd row** K(3D, 1Q) to end.
**33rd row** P(1Q, 3D) to end.
**34th–37th rows** Rep 32nd–33rd rows twice.
**38th row** As 32nd row.
**39th row** As 15th row reading 'D and Q' for 'C'.

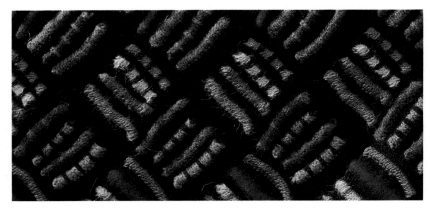

*(Opposite) There isn't a pattern for this cardigan, but it's actually a smaller version of the interlace Kimono worked in peachy, heathery tones.*

**40th–43rd rows** As 4th–7th rows.
**44th–51st rows** As 32nd–39th rows using E instead of D, and L instead of Q.
Rep 2nd–3rd rows until all sts from first rectangle have been worked off.*** One rectangle in the second row of rectangles has now been completed. Leave these sts on right-hand needle.*** Rep from *** to *** 13 times more but work 1st row as 'P up 16 sts along side of first rectangle, turn', to make 14 rectangles in all.
Work third row of rectangles as for first row but in each rectangle use F instead of B for first 'piped cord', G instead of H and A for second 'piped cord', R and S instead of J and L for third 'piped cord', and C instead of M and A for fourth 'piped cord'.
Work fourth row of rectangles as for second row but in each rectangle use (3S, 1A) 4 times instead of C for first 'piped cord', (3D, 1A) 4 times instead of N for second 'piped cord', E and F instead of D and Q for third 'piped cord', and G instead of E and L for fourth 'piped cord'.
These four rows of rectangles form the patt rep.
Cont in patt until 9 rows of rectangles have been worked in all.
**Divide for armholes**
Keeping patt correct (as a 2nd rectangle row) work 3 rectangles for left front, then cast off for armhole as foll:
**1st row** With A, P up 15 sts along side of rectangle, turn.
**2nd row** K16.

**3rd row** P2 tog, P13, P2 tog (using 1st st of next rectangle), turn.
**4th row** K15.
**5th row** P2 tog, P12, P2 tog, turn.
**6th row** K14.
**7th row** P2 tog, P11, P2 tog.
**8th row** K13.
**9th row** P2 tog, P10, P2 tog, turn.
**10th row** K12.
**11th row** P2 tog, P9, P2 tog, turn.
**12th row** K11.
**13th row** P2 tog, P8, P2 tog, turn.
**14th row** K10.
**15th row** P2 tog, P7, P2 tog, turn.
**16th row** K9.
**17th row** P2 tog, P6, P2 tog, turn.
**18th row** K8.
**19th row** P2 tog, P5, P2 tog, turn.
**20th row** K7.
**21st row** P2 tog, P4, P2 tog, turn.
**22nd row** K6.
**23rd row** P2 tog, P3, P2 tog, turn
**24th row** K5.
**25th row** P2 tog, P2, P2 tog, turn.
**26th row** K4.
**27th row** P2 tog, P1, P2 tog, turn.
**28th row** K3.
**29th row** (P2 tog) twice, turn.
**30th row** K2.
**31st row** P2 tog, P1, turn.
**32nd row** S1 1, K1, psso. 1 st rem.
Now work 6 rectangles keeping patt correct for back, then cast off for second armhole by working 1st–30th rows as before. Keeping patt correct, work 3 rectangles to complete row for right front.
Leave sts of left front and back on spare needles and cont on sts for right front only.
Work 2 rows of rectangles.
**Shape front neck**
Cont in A only, omit selvedge triangle at front edge by casting off 16 sts of first rectangle – 1 st rem on right-hand needle.
**Next row** K up 15 sts along side of rectangle, turn. 16 sts.
Commencing with a rectangle, cont in patt (as 1st rectangle row) to end. Work 1 more rectangle row.
Cast off for shoulder by working triangles as foll:
Cast off 16 sts of first rectangle – 1 st rem on right-hand needle.
**Next row** K up 17 sts along side of rectangle, turn. 18 sts.
**Next row** P18.
**Next row** K2 tog, K15, sl 1, K1 (using 1 st from next rectangle), psso, turn.
**Next row** P17.
**Next row** K2 tog, K14, sl 1, K1, psso, turn.
**Next row** P16.
Cont in this way until the row '(K2 tog) twice,' has been worked, pass 1st st over 2nd st – 1 st rem on right-hand needle.
**Work left half triangle**
Work as given for cast-off for armhole, reading K for P and P for K throughout. Fasten off last st.
With rs of work facing return to sts for back, keeping patt correct work 4 rows of rectangles.
Cast off as foll:
**Right half triangle**
Cont in A only.
**1st row** K2, turn.
**2nd row** P2.
**3rd row** K into front and back of next st, sl 1, K1, psso, turn.
**4th row** P3.
**5th row** K into front and back of next st, K1, sl 1, K1, psso, turn.

**6th row** P4.
**7th row** K into front and back of next st, K2, sl 1, K1, psso, turn.
**8th row** P5.
**9th row** K into front and back of next st, K3, sl 1, K1, psso, turn.
**10th row** P6.
**11th row** K into front and back of next st, K4, sl 1, K1, psso, turn.
**12th row** P7.
**13th row** K into front and back of next st, K5, sl 1, K1, psso, turn.
**14th row** P8.
**15th row** K into front and back of next st, K6, sl 1, K1, psso, turn.
**16th row** P9.
**17th row** Sl 1, K1, psso, K6, sl 1, K1, psso, turn.
**18th row** P8.
**19th row** Sl 1, K1, psso, K5, sl 1, K1, psso, turn.
**20th row** P7.
**21st row** Sl 1, K1, psso, K4, sl 1, K1, psso, turn.
**22nd row** P6.
**23rd row** Sl 1, K1, psso, K3, sl 1, K1, psso, turn.
**24th row** P5.
**25th row** Sl 1, K1, psso, K2, sl 1, K1, psso, turn.
**26th row** P4.
**27th row** Sl 1, K1, psso, K1, sl 1, K1, psso, turn.
**28th row** P3.
**29th row** (Sl 1, K1, psso) twice, pass 1st st over 2nd st – 1 st rem on right-hand needle.
Now complete casting off as given for right front shoulder.
With rs of work facing, return to sts for left front and complete to match right front, reversing shaping by omitting corresponding sections and working appropriate half triangles on cast-off row.

## SLEEVES
Using 3mm (US2) needles and yarn A, cast on 64 sts.
Work 13cm (5in) in K2 tbl, P2 rib.
Cont in rib, inc 1 st at each end of every row until there are 80 sts.
Change to 3¼mm (US3) needles and work in patt as for back and fronts, but working on a base row of 4 triangles until 9 rows of rectangles have been completed.
Cast off as given for back.

## GUSSETS
With rs of work facing, using 3¼mm (US3) needles and yarn A, K up 24 sts across cast-off sts at underarm.
Work in K1, P1 rib, dec 1 st at each end of every alt row until 2 sts rem.
Work 2 tog. Fasten off.

## TO MAKE UP
Join shoulder seams.
**Front band**
Using 3mm (US2) needles and yarn A, cast on 11 sts.
Work in K1 tbl, P1 rib until band when slightly stretched fits up right front, across back neck and down left front.
Cast off in rib.
Sew on front band.

## WELT
With rs of work facing, using 3mm (US2) circular needle and yarn A, K up 7 sts across front band, then K up 19 sts along bottom edge of each selvedge triangle, then 7 sts across front band. 280 sts. Work in rows.
K 4 rows. Cast off.
Place centre of cast-off edge of sleeves to shoulder seams and sew in place, joining sides of gussets to side seams. Join sleeve seams, reversing cuffs to fold back.

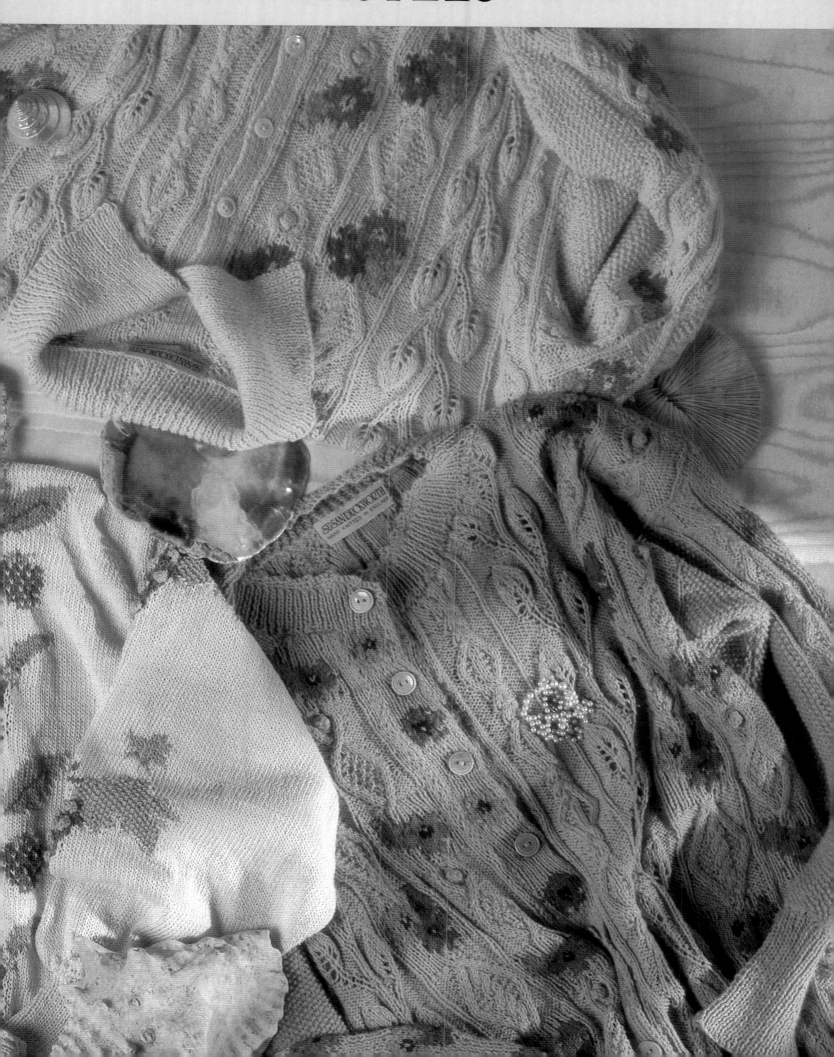

# *China Cardigan*

When I began this design I was simply attracted by the idea of filling circles with small-scale patterns like Liberty prints, but they ended up looking just like patterned china plates! This is a typical example of how delightfully removed the end product can be from the original source.

## SIZE
**To fit** one size only up to 91cm (36in) bust
**Actual width measurement** 104cm (41in)
**Length to shoulder** 65cm (25½in)
**Sleeve seam** 51cm (20in)

## MATERIALS
350g (13oz) Rowan Fine Fleck Tweed in natural 1 (A)
50g (2oz) each in terracotta tweed 21 (B), rose tweed 410 (C) and cobalt 51 (V)
50g (2oz) Rowan Botany Wool each in pewter 636 (D), bright lilac 70 (E), clover 94 (F), petrol 65 (G), blue moon 49 (H), coral 631 (J), marshmallow 68 (L), peach 83 (M), aubergine 602 (N), loden 89 (Q), dark purple 99 (R), mauve 121 (S), apricot 14 (T) and dove 52 (U)
**Equivalent yarn** four-ply
1 pair each 3mm (US2) and 3¼mm (US3) needles
3mm (US2) circular needle
Cable needle
16 buttons

*NOTE: A yarn kit is available for this design. See page 143 for details.*

*(Opposite) This version of the China Cardigan is the one provided in the kit. The mahogany colourway (below) looks great on strawberry blondes.*

## TENSION
30 sts and 40 rows to 10cm (4in) over patt on 3¼mm (US3) needles.

## SPECIAL ABBREVIATIONS
*cable 4* – sl next 2 sts on to cable needle and hold at front of work, K2, then K2 from cable needle.

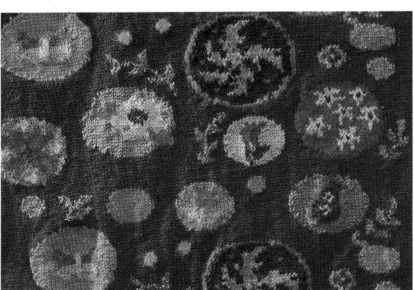

## BACK
Using 3mm (US2) needles and yarn A, cast on 156 sts.
Work 2cm (¾in) in K1 tbl, P1 rib.
Change to 3¼mm (US3) needles and work in cable rib as foll:
**1st row** (rs) (K4, P2) to end.
**2nd row** K all the P sts of previous row and P the K sts.
**3rd row** As 1st row.
**4th row** As 2nd row.
**5th row** (K4, P2, cable 4, P2) to end.
**6th row** As 2nd row.
The 1st–6th rows form patt rep.
Work 56 rows more in cable rib.
Now beg colour patt from chart 1, working in st st throughout and using separate lengths of yarn for each colour area, twisting yarns tog at colour joins to avoid holes, as foll:
**1st row** K21A, patt 1st row of chart, K21A.
**2nd row** P21A, patt 2nd row of chart, P21A.
These 2 rows set chart position.
Cont in patt until back measures 45cm (17¾in) from cast-on edge, ending with a ws row.
**Shape raglans**
** Dec 1 st at each end of next 3 rows.
Work 1 row.**
Rep from ** to ** 19 times more. 36 sts.
Cast off.

## LEFT FRONT
Using 3mm (US2) needles and yarn A, cast on 96 sts.
Work 2cm (¾in) in K1 tbl, P1 rib.
Change to 3¼mm (US3) needles and work 62 rows in cable rib as given for back, ending with a ws row.
Now work in colour patt from chart 1 between left front markers, until left front matches back to beg of raglan shaping, ending with a ws row.
**Shape raglan armhole**
***Next row K2 tog, patt to end. 95 sts.
**Next row** Patt to last 2 sts, P2 tog. 94 sts.
**Next row** K2 tog, patt to end. 93 sts.
Work 1 row. ***
Rep from *** to *** 18 times, *at the same time*, dec 1 st at neck edge on next and foll 34 alt rows. 4 sts.
**Next row** K2 tog, K2. 3 sts.
**Next row** P1, P2 tog. 2 sts
**Next row** K2 tog.
Fasten off.

## RIGHT FRONT
Using 3mm (US2) needles and yarn A, cast on 96 sts.
Work 2cm (¾in) in K1, P1 rib.
Change to 3¼mm (US3) needles and work in cable rib as for back, *at the same time* make buttonholes on 1st–2nd rows as foll:
**1st buttonhole row** Patt 34 sts, cast off 3 sts, patt to end.
**2nd buttonhole row** Patt to end, casting on 3 sts over those cast off in previous row.
Now work 60 rows more in cable rib, making buttonholes as before on 21st–22nd, 41st–42nd and 61st–62nd rows, ending with a ws row.
Now work in colour patt from chart 1 between right front markers, *at the same time* place pocket as foll:

**Divide for pocket**

**Next row** (rs) Patt 76 sts, turn, leaving rem sts on a spare needle, and cont on these sts only for right side of pocket.

Now work straight *at the same time* make buttonholes as before at 20-row intervals until 43 rows in chart patt have been worked, thus ending with a rs row.

Leave these sts on a spare needle.

With rs of work facing, return to sts on first spare needle, rejoin yarn and patt to end. 20 sts.

Now work 42 rows straight, thus ending with a rs row.

**Next row** Patt to end across these 20 sts, then patt to end across 76 sts left on second spare needle to join both sides of front. 96 sts.

Now complete to match left front making buttonholes at 20-row intervals as before until 8 buttonholes in all have been made, and reversing all shapings.

**SLEEVES**

Using 3mm (US2) needles and yarn A, cast on 52 sts. Work 18.5cm (7in) in K1 tbl, P1 rib.

**Next row** (Rib 1, rib twice into next st) to end. 78 sts. Change to 3¼mm (US3) needles and work in colour patt from chart 1 between sleeve markers, *at the same time* inc 1 st at each end of next and every foll 3rd row until there are 140 sts. Now work straight until sleeve measures 51cm (20in) from cast-on edge.

**Shape top**

****Dec 1 st at each end of next 4 rows. Work 1 row. Dec 1 st at each end of next 3 rows.****

Rep from **** to **** 9 times more. Fasten off.

**LEFT FRONT BAND**

Using 3mm (US2) needles and yarn A, cast on 11 sts. Work in K1 tbl, P1 rib until band when slightly

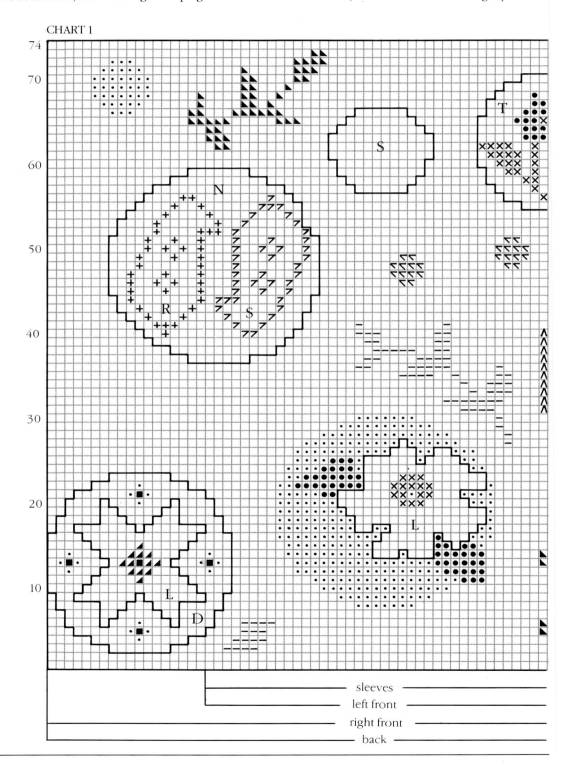

CHART 1

- sleeves ——————
- left front ——————
- right front ——————
- back ——————

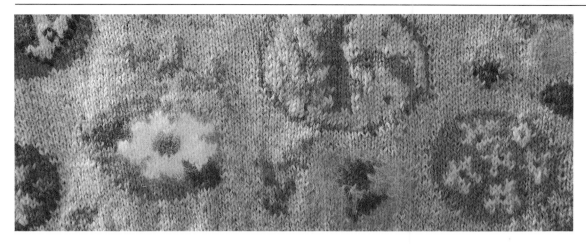

rep 1st – 74th rows

□ = A unless otherwise
     indicated

⊡ = B
◪ = C
◼ = D
◪ = E
● = F
▲ = G
◹ = H
⊠ = J
▼ = L
Ⅱ = M
⊟ = Q
◪ = R
⊞ = S
Ⅱ = T
◹ = U
◣ = V

sleeves
left front
right front
back

## CHART 2

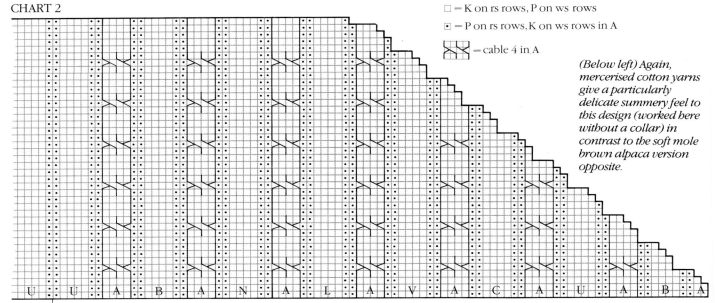

□ = K on rs rows, P on ws rows

⊡ = P on rs rows, K on ws rows in A

= cable 4 in A

*(Below left) Again, mercerised cotton yarns give a particularly delicate summery feel to this design (worked here without a collar) in contrast to the soft mole brown alpaca version opposite.*

U ⠄ U ⠄ A ⠄ B ⠄ A ⠄ N ⠄ A ⠄ L ⠄ A ⠄ V ⠄ A ⠄ C ⠄ A ⠄ U ⠄ A ⠄ B ⠄ A

centre line: reverse chart from this point

stretched, fits up left front edge to beg of neck shaping. Cast off in rib.

### RIGHT FRONT BAND

Work as for left front band, *at the same time* make 8 buttonholes to correspond with those on right front:
**1st buttonhole row** Rib 3, cast off 3 sts, rib to end.
**2nd buttonhole row** Rib to end, casting on 3 sts over those cast off in previous row.

### COLLAR

Using 3mm (US2) circular needle and yarn A, cast on 192 sts. Work in rows. Work 7 rows in K1 tbl, P1 rib. Now work in coloured cable rib from chart 2, using separate lengths of yarn for each colour area, twisting yarns tog at colour joins to avoid holes as foll:
**1st row** (rs) Sl 1, K3 tog, psso, work 93 sts from 1st row of chart reading from right to left to centre line, work 93 sts from 1st row of chart reading from left to right, K2 tog tbl, K3 tog tbl.
**2nd row** (ws) Work from 2nd row of chart reading from right to left to centre line, work 2nd row of chart reading from left to right.
**3rd row** K2 tog, work 3rd row of chart to centre line, work 3rd row of chart in reverse, K2 tog tbl.
**4th row** P2 tog, work 4th row of chart to centre line, work 4th row of chart in reverse, P2 tog tbl.
Rep last 4 rows until 92 sts rem.
Cast off 4 sts at beg of next 2 rows. 84 sts. Cast off.

### POCKET LINING

Using 3¼mm (US3) needles and yarn A, cast on 40 sts, then with rs facing K up 40 sts along left-hand edge of pocket opening. 80 sts.
Work 11cm (4¼in) in st st, beg with a P row. Cast off.

### POCKET EDGING

With rs of work facing, using 3mm (US2) needles and yarn A, K up 40 sts along front edge of pocket opening. Work 8 rows in K1 tbl, P1 rib. Cast off in rib.

### TO MAKE UP

Join raglan seams. Join side and sleeve seams.
Join cast-off edge of collar to neck edge.
Join on front bands, stretching them slightly to fit.
Catch down pocket linings and edgings.
Sew 8 buttons on to left front band opposite button-holes on right front, and sew 8 buttons on to left front opposite buttonholes on right front band.

# *Hyacinth*

Blocks of stocking stitch and hyacinth stitch are used here to make a simple, lacy summer sweater. One of my favourite versions of this design was made in fine cashmere, but any four-ply wool would work equally well.

## SIZES
**To fit** 86[91,96] cm (34[36,38]in) bust
**Actual width measurements** 94[97.5,101]cm (37[38½,40]in)
**Length to shoulder** 62[65,67]cm (24½[25,26¼]in)
**Sleeve seam** 43cm (17in)

## MATERIALS
350[350,400]g (13[13,15]oz) four-ply mercerised cotton in main colour (A)
50g (2oz) in contrast colour (B)
25g (1oz) in each of 10 contrast colours (C,D,E,F,G,H,J,L,M,N)
1 pair each 3mm (US2) and 3¼mm (US3) needles
1 set of four double-pointed 3mm (US2) needles
1 2.50mm (USC) crochet hook

## TENSION
34 sts and 34 rows to 10cm (4in) over hyacinth patt on 3mm (US2) and 3¼mm (US3) needles (two needles sizes are needed to work the patt).

## SPECIAL ABBREVIATION
*5 from 1* = (K1, P1, K1, P1, K1) into next st.

## BACK
Using 3mm (US2) needles and yarn A, cast on 120[126,132] sts.
Work 10[13,15.5]cm (4[5,6]in) in K1 tbl, P1 rib.
**Next row** K0[3,6], (K into front and back of next st, K2) to last 0[3,6] sts, K to end. 160[166,172] sts.
Now beg hyacinth patt, using 3mm (US2) needles for ws rows and 3¼mm (US3) needles for rs rows (use separate lengths of yarn for each colour area and twist yarns tog at colour joins to avoid holes).
**1st row** (ws) P1[2,1], *5 from 1 P5 tog; rep from * to last 3[2,3] sts, P3[2,3].
**2nd row** P to end.
**3rd row** P18[21,24]A, *P1B, with B (P5 tog, 5 from 1) 3 times, P1B, P6A; rep from * to last 38[41,44] sts, P1B, with B (P5 tog, 5 from 1) 3 times, P1B, P18[21,24]A.
**4th row** K18[21,24]A, *P20B, K6A; rep from * to last 12[15,18] sts, K to end in A.
**5th row** P18[21,24]A, *P1C, with C (5 from 1, P5 tog) 3 times, P1C, P6A; rep from * to last 38[41,44] sts, P1C, with C (5 from 1, P5 tog) 3 times, P1C, P18[21,24]A.
**6th row** As 4th row, using yarn C instead of yarn B.
**7th row** P18[21,24]A, * K20C, P6A; rep from * to last 12[15,18] sts, P to end in A.
**8th row** As 4th row, using yarn C instead of yarn B.
**9th–10th rows** As 3rd–4th rows, using yarn D instead of yarn B.
**11th–14th rows** As 5th–8th rows, using yarn E instead of yarn C.
**15th–16th rows** As 3rd–4th rows, using yarn F instead of yarn B.

**17th–20th rows** As 5th–8th rows, using yarn G instead of yarn C.
**21st–22nd rows** As 3rd–4th rows, using yarn H instead of yarn B.
**23rd–24th rows** As 1st–2nd rows.
**25th row** With yarn A, P1[2,1], (P5 tog, 5 from 1) to last 3[2,3] sts, P3[2,3].
**26th row** P to end in A.
**27th–30th rows** As 23rd–26th rows.
**31st–32nd rows** As 1st–2nd rows.
**33rd row** P31[34,37]A, *P1J, with J (5 from 1, P5 tog) 3 times, P1J, P6A; rep from * to last 51[54,57] sts, P1J, with J (5 from 1, P5 tog), P1J, P31[34,37]A.
**34th row** K31[34,37]A, *P20J, K6A; rep from * to last 25[28,31] sts, K to end in A.
**35th row** P31[34,37]A, P1B, with B (P5 tog, 5 from 1) 3 times, P1B, P6A; rep from * to last 51[54,57] sts, P1B, with B (P5 tog, 5 from 1), P1B, P31[34,37]A.
**36th row** As 34th row, using B instead of J.
**37th row** P31[34,37]A, *K20B, P6A; rep from * to last 25[28,31] sts, P to end in A.
**38th row** As 34th row, using yarn B instead of yarn J.
**39th–40th rows** As 33rd–34th rows, using yarn E instead of yarn J.
**41st–44th rows** As 35th–38th rows, using yarn L instead of yarn B.
**45th–46th rows** As 33rd–34th rows, using yarn M instead of yarn J.
**47th–50th rows** As 35th–38th rows, using yarn G instead of yarn B.
**51st–52nd rows** As 33rd–34th rows, using yarn N instead of yarn J.
**53rd–60th rows** As 23rd–30th rows.
Now rep 1st–60th rows foll colour sequence table for contrast colours (yarn A is worked as before), *at the same time* shape armholes on 31st row as foll:
**Shape armholes**
Keeping patt correct, cast off 8 sts at beg of next 2 rows. 144[150,156] sts.
Cont as set until 120 rows have been worked in hyacinth patt.**
Now rep 1st–56th rows again. Cast off.

## FRONT
Work as given for back to **.
Now rep 1st–31st rows.
**Divide for neck**
**Next row** Patt 48[51,54] sts, turn, leaving rem sts on a spare needle and cont on these sts only for first side of neck.
**Next row** P5A, P1J, with J (5 from 1, P5 tog) 3 times, P1J, P23[26,29]A.
**Next row** K23[26,29]A, P20J, K5A.
The last 2 rows set position of hyacinth patt. Cont as set working contrast colours as for back, until front matches back to cast-off row. Cast off.
With rs of work facing, return to sts on spare needle, rejoin yarn to next st, cast off 48 sts, patt to end. 48[51,54] sts.
Complete second side of neck to match first, reversing hyacinth patt.

## SLEEVES
Working from sleeve top down to cuff, using 3mm

(US2) needles and yarn A, cast on 172 sts. K 1 row.
Now work in hyacinth patt as given for 3rd size of back but working centre 3 panels only on 2nd patt rep, *at the same time* dec 1 st at each end of next and every foll 4th row until 128 sts rem.
Now work straight until 90 rows in all have been worked in hyacinth patt, ending with a ws row.

**Shape cuff**
Change to 3mm (US2) needles.
**Next row** With A (K2 tog) to end. 64 sts.
Work in K1 tbl, P1 rib until cuff measures 19cm (7½in). Cast off in rib.

**TO MAKE UP**
Join shoulder seams.
**Neckband**
Using double-pointed 3mm (US2) needles and yarn A, beg at left back neck, K up 26 sts down left front neck, 1 st from corner (mark this st), 47 sts across front neck, 1 st from corner (mark this st), 26 sts up right front neck and 47 sts across back neck. 148 sts.
**1st round** (K1, P1) 12 times, sl 1, K1, psso, P marked st, K2 tog, P1, (K1, P1) 21 times, sl 1, K1, psso, P marked st, K2 tog, P1, (K1, P1) to end.
**2nd round** Work in rib as set.

Work 6 more rounds, dec as before either side of marked sts on next and foll alt rows.
Cast off in rib, dec on cast-off row as before.
Set sleeves in flat, matching centre of cast-off edge to shoulder seam, and joining first few rows of sleeve to cast-off sts at underarm. Join side and sleeve seams.
**Crochet collar edging**
Using 2.50mm (USC) crochet hook and yarn A, work picot edging as foll:
**1st row** Work in double crochet around neck edge.
**2nd row** * 1 double crochet into each of next 3 double crochet, 4 chain, slipstitch into last double crochet; rep from * around neck edge. Fasten off.

**Colour sequence table**

| row | contrast | row | contrast |
| --- | --- | --- | --- |
| 61–62 | – | 93–94 | N |
| 63–64 | D | 95–98 | J |
| 65–68 | H | 99–100 | B |
| 69–70 | E | 101–104 | D |
| 71–74 | B | 105–106 | E |
| 75–76 | C | 107–110 | L |
| 77–80 | G | 111–112 | H |
| 81–82 | F | 113–120 | – |
| 83–92 | – | | |

*Hyacinth stitch gives this design a lacy, openwork feel.*

# *Marshmallow*

This is my adaptation of traditional Fair Isle. The single rows of blackberry stitch between the patterned bands and the sugary pastel cottons totally transform the character of the classic woollen pullovers.

## SIZES
**To fit** 81[91,96]cm (32[36,38]in) bust
**Actual width measurements** 86.5[96,101]cm (34[38,40]in)
**Length to shoulder** 62.5[66,71]cm (24½[26,28]in)
**Sleeve seam** 43[46,51.5]cm (17[18¼,20¼]in)

## MATERIALS
300[350,400]g (11[13,15]oz) four-ply mercerised cotton in main colour (A)
50g (2oz) in each of 2 contrast colours (B,C)
25g (1oz) in each of 9 contrast colours (D,E,F,G,H,J,L,M,N)
1 pair each 3mm (US2) and 3¼mm (US3) needles
1 2.50mm (USC) crochet hook

## TENSION
30 sts and 34 rows to 10cm (4in) over patt on 3¼mm (US3) needles.

## SPECIAL INSTRUCTIONS
**Blackberry Stitch**
(For back and front)
**1st row** (ws) K1[0,0], *P3 tog, (K1, P1, K1) into next st, rep from * to last 1[0,0] sts, K1[0,0].
**2nd row** P to end.
**3rd row** K1[0,0], *(K1, P1, K1) into next st, P3 tog; rep from * to last 1[0,0] sts, K1[0,0].
**4th row** P to end.
These 4 rows form the patt rep.
For sleeve, work as given for 2nd and 3rd sizes of back and front.

## BACK
Using 3mm (US2) needles and yarn A, cast on 130[144,152] sts.
Work 7cm (2¾in) in K1 tbl, P1 rib, ending with a rs row.
Change to 3¼mm (US3) needles and beg colour patt as foll (work in st st unless otherwise indicated):

CHART 2   □ = D     sleeve: beg rs rows
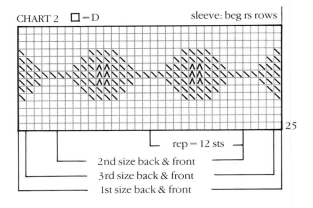
25
rep = 12 sts
2nd size back & front
3rd size back & front
1st size back & front

CHART 3   □ = A     sleeve: beg rs rows
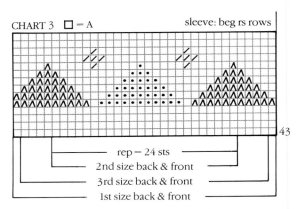
43
rep = 24 sts
2nd size back & front
3rd size back & front
1st size back & front

CHART 4   □ = E     sleeve: beg rs rows
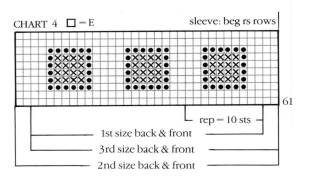
61
rep = 10 sts
1st size back & front
3rd size back & front
2nd size back & front

☑ = C
Ⅶ = F
☒ = G
◉ = J
⊡ = L
◪ = M
◩ = N

CHART 1   □ = A     sleeve: beg rs rows
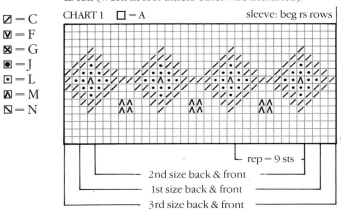
5
rep = 9 sts
2nd size back & front
1st size back & front
3rd size back & front

CHART 5   □ = B     sleeve: beg rs rows
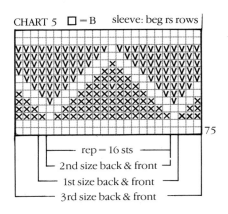
75
rep = 16 sts
2nd size back & front
1st size back & front
3rd size back & front

**1st–4th rows** With yarn B, work in blackberry st.
**5th–20th rows** Beg with a P row, work in patt from chart 1.
**21st–24th rows** With yarn C, work in blackberry st.
**25th–38th rows** Beg with a P row, work in patt from chart 2.
**39th–42nd rows** With yarn E, work in blackberry st.
**43rd–56th rows** Beg with a P row, work in patt from chart 3.
**57th–60th rows** With yarn B, work in blackberry st.

**61st–70th rows** Beg with a P row, work in patt from chart 4.
**71st–74th rows** With yarn H, work in blackberry st.
**75th–88th rows** Beg with a P row, work in patt from chart 5. These 88 rows form the patt rep.
Cont in patt until back measures 41[43,46]cm (16[17,18]in) from cast-on edge, ending with a ws row.
**Shape armholes**
Keeping patt correct, cast off 8 sts at beg of next 2 rows. 114[128,136] sts.**
Now work straight until back measures 21.5[23,25]cm (8½[9,9¾]in) from beg of armhole shaping, ending with a ws row.
**Shape shoulders**
Cast off 11[13,14] sts at beg of next 6 rows. 48[50,52] sts. Cast off.

**FRONT**
Work as given for back to **.
Now work straight until front measures 14 rows less than back to beg of shoulder shaping, ending with a ws row.
**Divide for neck**
**Next row** Patt 43[50,54] sts, turn, leaving rem sts on a spare needle, and cont on these sts only for first side of neck.
Dec 1 st at neck edge on every row until there are 33[40,42] sts, then work straight until front matches back to shoulder, ending at armhole edge.
**Shape shoulder**
Cast off 11[13,14] sts at beg of next and every foll alt row.
Work 1 row.
Cast off.
With rs facing, return to sts on spare needle rejoin yarn to next st, cast off centre 28 sts, patt to end. 43[50,54] sts.
Now complete second side of neck to match first side, reversing shapings.

**SLEEVES**
Using 3mm (US2) needles and yarn A, cast on 64 sts.
Work 10cm (4in) in K1 tbl, P1 rib.
**Next row** (P twice into next st, P1) to end. 96 sts.
**Next row** K to end.
Change to 3¼mm (US3) needles and work in colour patt as given for back, *at the same time* inc 1 st at each end of next and every foll 3rd row until there are 130[140,150] sts, working the extra sts into patt.
Now work straight until sleeve measures 46[49,54]cm (18¼[19¼,21¼]in) from cast-on edge, ending with a ws row.
Cast off.

**COLLAR**
Join shoulder seams.
Using 3¼mm (US3) needles and yarn A, cast on 20 sts.
Work in blackberry st as given for 2nd and 3rd size of back until collar is long enough to fit around neck edge, ending on a 2nd or 4th patt row.
Cast off.

**TO MAKE UP**
Join on collar to neck edge so that short ends of collar meet neatly at centre front.
**Crochet collar edging**
Using 2.50mm (USC) crochet hook and yarn A, beg at centre front, work shell edging around collar as foll: 2 double crochet, *(2 double crochet, 1 chain, 2 double crochet) all into next st, 2 double crochet; rep from * to end.
Set in sleeves in flat, matching centre of cast-off edge to shoulder seam, and joining last few rows to cast-off sts at underarm.
Join side and sleeve seams.

# *Aran Floral*

This is a dainty version of the chunky traditional Aran cable stitches. The lightweight cotton yarn and stylized flowers help create a pretty summer cardigan.

## SIZE

**To fit** one size only up to 96cm (38in) bust
**Actual width measurement** 104cm (41in)
**Length to shoulder** 58cm (22¾in)
**Sleeve seam** 49cm (19¼in)

## MATERIALS

450g (16oz) four-ply cotton in main colour (A)
25g (1oz) in each of 5 contrast colours (B,C,D,E,F)
1 pair each 3mm (US2) and 3¼mm (US3) needles
Cable needle
8 buttons

## TENSION

33 sts and 37 rows to 10cm (4in) over patt unstretched on 3¼mm (US3) needles.

## SPECIAL ABBREVIATIONS

*make 1* – pick up loop between last st and next st and K it tbl
*make bobble* – (K1, P1, K1, P1, K1) into next st, turn, K5, turn, P5, turn, K5, turn, P5 tog.

*FC (front cross)* – sl next 2 sts on to cable needle and hold at front of work, P1, then K2 from cable needle
*BC (back cross)* – sl next st on to cable needle and hold at back of work, K2, then P1 from cable needle
*cable 4 front* – sl next 2 sts on to cable needle and hold at front of work, K2, then K2 from cable needle
*cable 4 back* – sl next 2 sts on to cable needle and hold at back of work, K2, then K2 from cable needle
*BKC (back knit cross)* – as BC but K all sts
*FKC (front knit cross)* – as FC but K all sts
*RT (right twist)* – sl next 3 sts on to cable needle and hold at back of work, K2, then sl P st from cable needle back on to left-hand needle and P it, then K2 from cable needle

## CABLE PANELS

Ravelled braid cable, rope and diamond cable and Aran bobbled cable are shown on chart 1 *and* given in the following written instructions. Twining leaf patt is given only as written instructions. Follow chart 1 for layout of cable panels and colour patt.

**Rope and diamond cable**
Worked over 18 sts.
**1st row** (ws) K7, P4, K7.
**2nd row** P6, BKC, FKC, P6.
**3rd row** K6, P2, K2, P2, K6.
**4th row** P5, BKC, K2, FKC, P5.
**5th and every alt row** K the P sts of previous row and P the K sts, *except* on each side of cable within

|  |  |
|---|---|
| ⊡ = | P on rs rows, K on ws rows in A |
| □ = | A |
| ◣ = | B |
| ☒ = | C |
| ◪ = | D |
| ▨ = | E |
| ⊟ = | F |

K on rs rows, P on ws rows

o = make bobble in A

⫴ = right twist (RT)

⫽ = back knit cross (BKC)

⫻ = front knit cross (FKC)

⫽ = cable 4 back

⫻ = cable 4 front

⫽ = back cross (BC)

⫻ = front cross (FC)

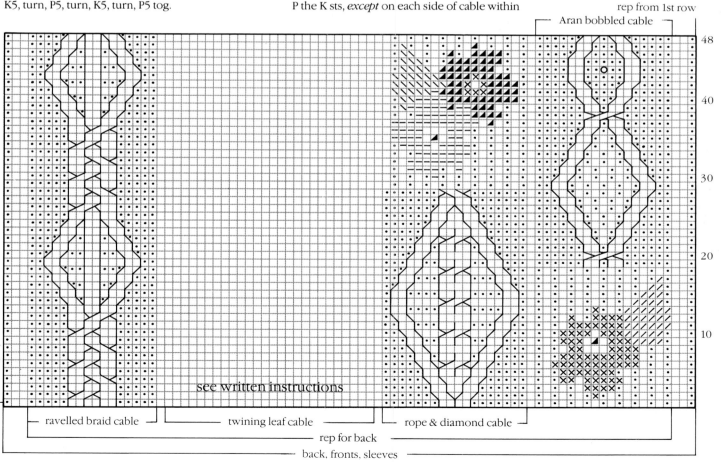

Aran bobbled cable

rep from 1st row

48

40

30

20

10

1st row (ws)

see written instructions

ravelled braid cable — twining leaf cable — rope & diamond cable

rep for back

back, fronts, sleeves

diamond where all sts are K on rs and ws rows.
**6th row** P4, BKC, cable 4 back, FKC, P4.
**8th row** P3, BKC, K6, FKC, P3.
**10th row** P2, BKC, K2, cable 4 back, K2, FKC, P2.
**12th row** P1, BKC, K10, FKC, P1.
**14th row** P1, K6, cable 4 back, K6, P1.
**16th row** P1, FC, K10, BC, P1.
**18th row** P2, FC, K2, cable 4 back, K2, BC, P2.
**20th row** P3, FC, K6, BC, P3.
**22nd row** P4, FC, cable 4 back, BC, P4.
**24th row** P5, FC, K2, BC, P5.
**26th row** P6, FC, BC, P6.
**28th row** P7, cable 4 front, P7.
These 28 rows form rope and diamond cable panel.

### Twining leaf patt
Worked over 26 sts, (but sts are made and lost during patt rows).
**1st row** (ws) K5, P5, K4, P3, K9
**2nd row** P7, P2 tog, K into front and back of next st, K2, P4, K2, yo, K1, yo, K2, P5.
**3rd row** K5, P7, K4, P2, K1, P1, K8.
**4th row** P6, P2 tog, K1, P into front and back of next st, K2, P4, K3, yo, K1, yo, K3, P5.
**5th row** K5, P9, K4, P2, K2, P1, K7.
**6th row** P5, P2 tog, K1, P into front and back of next st, P1, K2, P4, sl 1, K1, psso, K5, K2 tog, P5.
**7th row** K5, P7, K4, P2, K3, P1, K6.
**8th row** P4, P2 tog, K1, P into front and back of next st, P2, K2, P4, sl 1, K1, psso, K3, K2 tog, P5.
**9th row** K5, P5, K4, P2, K4, P1, K5.
**10th row** P5, yo, K1, yo, P4, K2, P4, sl 1, K1, psso, K1, K2 tog, P5.
**11th row** K5, P3, K4, P2, K4, P3, K5.
**12th row** P5, (K1, yo) twice, K1, P4, K1, make 1, K1, P2 tog, P2, sl 2 K-wise, K1, p2sso, P5.
**13th row** K9, P3, K4, P5, K5.
**14th row** P5, K2, yo, K1, yo, K2, P4, K1, K into front and back of next st, K1, P2, tog, P7.
**15th row** K8, P1, K1, P2, K4, P7, K5.
**16th row** P5, K3, yo, K1, yo, K3, P4, K2, P into front and back of next st, K1, P2 tog, P6.
**17th row** K7, P1, K2, P2, K4, P9, K5.
**18th row** P5, sl 1, K1, psso, K5, K2 tog, P4, K2, P1, P into front and back of next st, K1, P2 tog, P5.
**19th row** K6, P1, K3, P2, K4, P7, K5.
**20th row** P5, sl 1, K1, psso, K3, K2 tog, P4, K2, P2, P into front and back of next st, K1, P2 tog, P4.
**21st row** K5, P1, K4, P2, K4, P5, K5.
**22nd row** P5, sl 1, K1, psso, K1, K2 tog, P4, K2, P4, yo, K1, yo, P5.
**23rd row** K5, P3, K4, P2, K4, P3, K5.
**24th row** P5, sl 2 K-wise, K1, p2sso, P2, P2 tog, K1, make 1, K1, P4, (K1, yo) twice, K1, P5.
These 24 rows form the patt rep (when working instructions always count this panel as 26 sts when making st checks).

### Ravelled braid cable
Worked over 16 sts.
**1st row** (ws) K5, P6, K5.
**2nd, 6th and 10th rows** P5, K2, cable 4 back, P5.
**3rd and every alt row** K the P sts of previous row and P the K sts.
**4th, 8th and 12th rows** P5, cable 4 front, K2, P5.
**14th row** P4, BC, K2, FC, P4.
**16th row** P3, BC, P1, K2, P1, FC, P3.
**18th row** P2, BC, P2, K2, P2, FC, P2.
**20th row** P2, FC, P2, K2, P2, BC, P2.
**22nd row** P3, FC, P1, K2, P1, BC, P3.
**24th row** P4, FC, K2, BC, P4.
These 24 rows form the ravelled braid cable patt rep.

### Aran bobbled cable
Worked over 17 sts.

**1st and 3rd rows** (ws) K6, P2, K1, P2, K6.
**2nd row** P6, RT, P6.
**4th row** P5, BC, K1, FC, P5.
**5th and every alt row** K the P sts of previous row and P the K sts.
**6th row** P4, BC, K1, P1, K1, FC, P4.
**8th row** P3, BC, (K1, P1) twice, K1, FC, P3.
**10th row** P2, BC, (K1, P1) 3 times, K1, FC, P2.
**12th row** P2, FC, (P1, K1) 3 times, P1, BC, P2.
**14th row** P3, FC, (P1, K1) twice, P1, BC, P3.
**16th row** P4, FC, P1, K1, P1, BC, P4.
**18th row** P5, FC, P1, BC, P5.
**20th row** As 2nd row.
**22nd row** P5, BC, P1, FC, P5.
**24th row** P4, BC, P3, FC, P4.
**26th row** P4, K2, P2, make bobble, P2, K2, P4.
**28th row** P4, FC, P3, BC, P4.
**30th row** As 18th row.
These 30 rows form Aran bobbled cable.

### RIGHT FRONT

Using 3mm (US2) needles and yarn A, cast on 87 sts.
K 1 row.
Work in lace rib as foll:
**1st row** (ws) K2, *P3 tog, K2; rep from * to end.
**2nd row** P2, *yo, P1, yo, P2; rep from * to end.
These 2 rows form lace rib patt rep.
Cont in lace rib until work measures 6cm (2½in) from cast-on edge, ending with a rs row (dec 1 st at end of last row). 86 sts.
Change to 3¼mm (US3) needles and work in cable and colour patt, using separate lengths of yarn for each st st colour area, twisting yarns tog at colour joins to avoid holes, as foll:
**1st row** (ws) K1, P2, K5, P6, K5, P1, K5, P5, K4, P3, K9, P1, K7, P4, K7, P1, (K1, P1) 8 times, K1, P2, K1.
**2nd row** Using A, P1, K2, (P1, K1) 4 times, P1, K1C,

using A (P1, K1) 3 times, P1, K1, P6, BKC, FKC, P6, K1, P7, P2 tog, K into front and back of next st, K2, P4, K2, yo, K1, yo, K2, P5, K1, P5, K2, cable 4 back, P5, K2, P1.
These 2 rows set position of cable panels and colour patt.
Cont as set, foll chart for colour patts and layout of cable panels, until 179 rows in all have been worked from chart, ending with a ws row.
**Shape neck**
Keeping patt correct, cast off 20 sts at beg of next row, then dec 1 st at neck edge on every row until 55 sts rem. Work 1 row straight (192 rows in all have been worked from chart). Cast off.

### LEFT FRONT

Work as given for right front, reversing shaping, by working 1 row less before neck shaping and 1 row extra before shoulder.

### BACK

Using 3mm (US2) needles and yarn A, cast on 167 sts.
K 1 row.
Work 6cm (2½in) in lace rib as given for right front, ending with a rs row (dec 1 st at centre of last row). 166 sts.
Change to 3¼mm (US3) needles and work in cable and floral patt foll chart for colour patt and layout of cable panels until 192 rows in all have been worked from chart.
Cast off.

### SLEEVES

Using 3mm (US2) needles and yarn A cast on 58 sts.
Work 10cm (4in) in K1, P1 rib.
**Next row** (P1, K into front and back of next st) 28 times, P1, K1. 86 sts.
Change to 3¼mm (US3) needles and work in cable and floral patt as for front, *at the same time* inc 1 st at each end of next and every foll 3rd row until there are 164 sts, working the extra sts in moss st.
Now work straight until 144 rows have been worked from chart. Cast off.

### BUTTON BAND

Using 3mm (US2) needles and yarn A, cast on 9 sts.
Work in K1, P1 rib until band when slightly stretched fits up left front edge, ending at inner edge.
Leave these sts on a safety pin.
Mark position of one button 2cm (¾in) from cast-on edge, one 2cm (¾in) from top edge and the rest spaced evenly between.

### BUTTONHOLE BAND

Work as for button band but ending at outer edge, making buttonholes to correspond with button markers as foll:
**1st buttonhole row** Rib 3, cast off 3 sts, rib to end.
**2nd buttonhole row** Rib to end, casting on 3 sts over those cast off in previous row.

### TO MAKE UP

Join shoulder seams.
Join on front bands, stretching slightly to fit.
**Collar**
With rs of work facing, using 3mm (US2) needles and yarn A, rib 9 across top of buttonhole band, K up 47 sts around right front neck, 55 sts across back neck, 47 sts around left front neck, and rib 9 across top of button band. 167 sts.
Work 9cm (3½in) in K1, P1 rib.
Cast off in rib.
Set in sleeves flat, matching centre of cast-off edge to shoulder seam.
Join side and sleeve seams.
Sew on buttons.

*(Below) The subdued mink woollen version of Aran Floral shows a ribbed floral cuff that I sometimes use on this design. The motif can easily be lifted from the chart. In the almond green colourway (right) the flowers are also worked up the front bands.*

# Cabbage Rose

Chintz fabrics from Liberty's were what I had in mind when working on this sweater. It's the kind of jumper that can be worn in many ways, either dressed up and extravagant or quietly classic, or elegantly, as here on a bench in the beautiful gardens of Parham House, Sussex.

## SIZES
**To fit** 91[97]cm (36[38]in) bust
**Actual width measurement** 100[106]cm (39½[41¾]in)
**Length to shoulder** 65[67.5]cm (25½[26½]in)
**Sleeve seam** 48cm (19in)

## MATERIALS
500[550]g (19[20]oz) Rowan Double Knitting Wool in black 62 (A)
50g (2oz) in each of seven contrast colours pale pink 68 (B), grape 69 (C), mauve 121 (D), shrimp 79 (E), loden 89 (F), apricot 23 (G) and terracotta 24 (H)
25g (1oz) in each of 5 contrast colours mulberry 70 (J), birch olive 59 (L), army green 407 (M), clover 602 (N) and cypress 90 (Q)
**Equivalent yarn** double knitting
1 pair each 3mm (US2) and 3¼mm (US3) needles
Set of four double-pointed 3mm (US2) needles

*NOTE: A yarn kit is available for this design. See page 143 for details.*

## TENSION
24 sts and 32 rows to 10cm (4in) over st st on 3¼mm (US3) needles.

## BACK
Using 3mm (US2) needles and yarn A, cast on 135[143] sts.
Work 4cm (1½in) in K1, P1 rib.
Change to 3¼mm (US3) needles and work 5cm (2in) in st st, ending with a P row.
Now cont in st st, work colour patt from chart 1, using separate lengths of yarn for each colour area, twisting yarns tog at colour joins to avoid holes.
Cont in patt, work 114 rows, ending with a ws row.
**Shape armholes**
Cast off 10 sts at beg of next 2 rows. 115[123] sts.**
Keeping chart patt correct, work straight until back measures 23[25.5]cm (9[10]in) from beg of armhole shaping, ending with a ws row (when chart 1 is complete, cont in A only)
**Shape shoulders**
Cast off 14[15] sts at beg of next 6 rows.
Leave rem 31[33] sts on a spare needle.

## FRONT
Work as given for back to **.
Now work straight until 14 rows less than back to

— 1st size —
— 2nd size —

CHART 1

☐ = A     ▲ = J
◉ = C     ⊡ = L
◩ = D     ⊞ = M
☑ = F     ■ = N
◪ = G     ⊠ = Q
◪ = H

shoulder shaping have been worked, ending with a ws row (when chart 1 is complete, cont in A only).

**Divide for neck**

**Next row** K46[49], turn, leaving rem sts on a spare needle and cont on these sts only for first side of neck. Dec 1 st at neck edge on every row until 42[45] sts rem.

Now work straight until front matches back to beg of shoulder shaping, ending at armhole edge.

**Shape shoulder**

Cast off 14[15] sts at beg of next and foll alt row.
Work 1 row.
Cast off.
With rs of work facing, return to sts on spare needle, rejoin yarn to next st, cast off 23[25] sts, patt to end. 46[49] sts.
Complete second side of neck to match first, reversing shapings.

CHART 2

□ = A
◉ = C
◤ = D
◿ = F
◺ = G
⋁ = H
◭ = J
▣ = L
⊞ = M
◼ = N
⊠ = Q

## SLEEVES

Using 3mm (US2) needles and yarn A, cast on 60 sts.
Work 10cm (4in) in K1, P1 rib.
**Next row** (Inc 1, rib 2) to end. 80 sts.
Change to 3¼mm (US3) needles and work in st st, inc
1 st at each end of every foll 4th row until there are 90
sts, end ws row. Beg colour patt from chart 2 as foll:
**Next row** K5A, patt 1st row of chart 2, K5A.
This row establishes position of chart 2.
Cont in patt, *at the same time* inc 1 st at each end of
every 4th row as set until there are 110[122] sts.
Work straight until sleeve measures 52cm (20in) from
cast-on edge, ending with a ws row (when chart 2 is
complete cont in A only). Cast off.

## TO MAKE UP

Join shoulder seams.
**Collar**
With rs of work facing, using double-pointed 3mm
(US2) needles and yarn A, beg at centre front, K up 37
sts around right front neck, K across 31[33] back neck
sts and K up 37 sts around left front neck. 105[107] sts.
Work in rows.
Work 8cm (3¼in) in K1, P1 rib.
Cast off in rib.
Set sleeves in flat, matching centre of cast-off edge to
shoulder seam and joining last few rows of sleeve to
cast-off sts at underarm.
Join side and sleeve seams.

*(Previous page) On the
grand staircase of
Polesden Lacey, near
Epsom, Surrey, from left
to right: Apple Branch
(page 106), Cabbage
Rose and Ellipses (page
112).*

# *Plum Blossom*

A designers' favourite – ginger jars – was the inspiration for this sweater. But instead of the usual blue and white, I decided to use Chinese lacquer colours, dark and rich, which makes the source much less obvious.

## SIZES
**To fit** 91[96,101]cm (36[38,40]in) bust
**Actual width measurements** 99[105,111]cm (39[41½,43¾]in)
**Length to shoulder** 67cm (26½in)
**Sleeve seam** 52cm (20½in)

## MATERIALS
400[450,500]g (15[17,19]oz) four-ply wool in main colour (A)
50g (2oz) in each of 10 contrast colours (B,C,D,E,F,G,H,J,L,M)
1 pair each 2¾mm (US2) and 3¼mm (US3) needles
3 buttons

## TENSION
32 sts and 36 rows to 10cm (4in) over st st on 3¼mm (US3) needles.

## BACK
Using 2¾mm (US2) needles and yarn A, cast on 158[168,178] sts. Work 13cm (5in) in K1, P1 rib.
Change to 3¼mm (US3) needles and beg colour patt from chart as foll:
**1st row** (rs) K19[24,29]A, (patt 1st row of chart) twice, K19[24,29]A.
**2nd row** P19[24,29]A, (patt 2nd row of chart) twice, P19[24,29]A.
These 2 rows set the position of the chart patt.
Cont in patt, working in st st throughout, until 30cm (11¾in) has been worked from top of rib.
**Shape armholes**
Keeping patt correct, cast off 5 sts at beg of next 2 rows. Dec 1 st at each end of next and every foll alt row until 138[148,158] sts rem.**
Now work straight until back measures 24cm (9½in) from beg of armhole shaping, ending with a ws row (194 rows of chart have now been completed).

*In this alternative colourway for Plum Blossom these rather weird colours are strangely pleasing.*

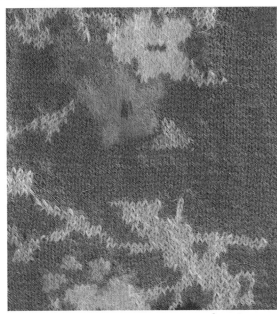

□ = A  ▲ = G
⊡ = B  ⧄ = H
⊞ = C  ▼ = J
☑ = D  ⊟ = L
⊠ = E  ⦿ = M
◩ = F

rep from 1st row

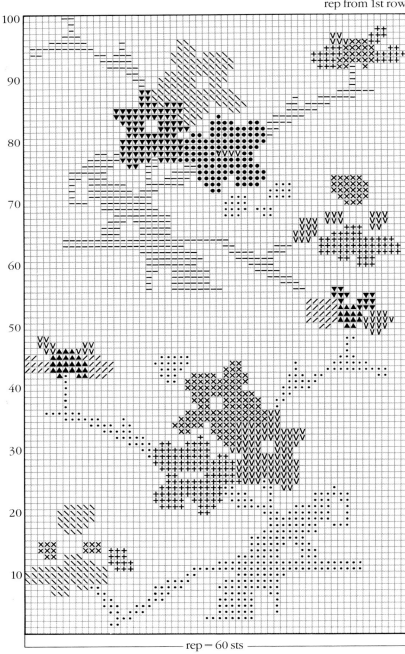

rep = 60 sts

### Shape shoulders
Cast off 12[14,16] sts at beg of next 4 rows, and 12[13,14] sts at beg of next 2 rows. 66 sts.
Cast off.

### FRONT
Work as given for back to **.
Now work straight until front measures 10 rows less than back to shoulder shaping, ending with a ws row.
### Divide for neck
**Next row** Patt 54[59,64] sts, turn, leaving rem sts on a spare needle and cont on these sts only for first side of neck.
**Next row** Sl 1, P2 tog, psso, patt to end.
**Next row** Patt to last 3 sts, K3 tog.
Rep these 2 rows until 36[41,46] sts rem, ending at armhole edge.
### Shape shoulder
Cast off 12[14,16] sts at beg of next and foll alt row. 12[13,14] sts. Work 1 row.
Cast off.
Return to sts on spare needle and, with rs of work facing, rejoin yarn to next st, cast off 30 sts, patt to end. 54[59,64] sts.
**Next row** Patt to end.
**Next row** Sl 1, K2 tog, psso, patt to end.
**Next row** Patt to last 3 sts, P3 tog tbl.
Complete second side of neck to match first side, reversing shapings.

### SLEEVES
Using 2¾mm (US2) needles and yarn A, cast on 60 sts.
Work 86 rows in K1, P1 rib, *at the same time* inc 1 st at each end of 14th and every foll 3rd row until there are 110 sts.
Change to 3¼mm (US3) needles and beg colour patt from chart as foll:
**1st row** (rs) K25A, patt 1st row of chart, K25A.
**2nd row** P25A, patt 2nd row of chart, P25A.
These 2 rows set the position of the chart patt.
Cont as set, working in st st throughout, inc 1 st at each end of next and every foll 3rd row until there are 144 sts (51 rows of chart have been completed).
Now work 37 rows straight, ending with a ws row (88 rows of chart have been completed).
### Shape top
Cast off 5 sts at beg of next 2 rows. Then dec 1 st at each end of next and every foll alt row until 124 sts rem, ending with a ws row (100 rows of chart have been completed).
Cast off.

### TO MAKE UP
Join right shoulder seam.
### Collar
Using 3¼mm (US3) needles and yarn A, K up 70 sts evenly from front neck edge and 50 sts across back neck to a point 1.5cm (½in) before left back shoulder edge. 120 sts.
Work 8cm (3in) in K1, P1 rib.
Cast off in rib.
### Collar edging
Using 3¼mm (US3) needles and yarn A, K up 20 sts along back neck opening of collar.
Work 5 rows in K1, P1 rib.
Cast off in rib.
Work a similar edging on front neck opening of collar, making 3 buttonholes on 3rd row as foll:
**Buttonhole row** Rib 3, (yo, K2 tog, rib 4) twice, yo, K2 tog, rib 3.
Join left shoulder seam to neck edge.
Set sleeves in flat, matching centre of cast-off edge to shoulder seam.
Join side seams.
Sew on buttons.

# Peacock

The idea of large motifs across this neat little sweater shape appealed very much to me. Then I balanced them with tiny flower sprigs on the sleeves. The peacocks were loosely based on an old black and white Chinese print.

## SIZE
**To fit** one size only up to 96cm (38in) bust
**Actual width measurement** 109cm (43in)
**Length to shoulder** 63cm (24¾in)
**Sleeve seam** 48cm (19in)

## MATERIALS
400g (15oz) four-ply wool in main colour (A)
50g (2oz) in each of 4 contrast colours (B,C,D,E)
25g (1oz) in each of 14 contrast colours
   (F,G,H,J,L,M,N,Q,R,S,T,U,V,W)
1 pair each 3mm (US2) and 3¼mm (US3) needles
1 2.50mm (USC) crochet hook
Cable needle
3 buttons

## TENSION
29 sts and 38 rows to 10cm (4in) over patt on 3¼mm (US3) needles.

## BACK
Using 3mm (US2) needles and yarn A, cast on 158 sts.
Work 2cm (¾in) in K1, P1 rib.
Change to 3¼mm (US3) needles and work in cable rib as foll:
**1st row** (rs) P2, (K4, P2) to end.
**2nd row** K all the K sts and P all the P sts of previous row.
**3rd row** As 1st row.
**4th row** As 2nd row.
**5th row** P2, *K4, P2, sl next 2 sts on to cable needle and hold at front of work, K2, then K2 from cable needle, P2; rep from * to end.
**6th row** As 2nd row.
These 6 rows form the cable rib patt rep.
Cont in cable rib until back measures 18cm (7in) from cast-on edge, ending with a ws row.
Beg colour patt from charts 1 and 2, working 30 sts across chart 1, then 98 sts across chart 2, then 30 sts across chart 1 again, using separate lengths of yarn for each colour area and twisting yarns tog at colour joins to avoid holes, as foll:
**1st row** (rs) K37A, 1B, 3A, 1B, 116A.
**2nd row** P115A, 3B, 2A, 1B, 37A.
These 2 rows establish the chart patt.
Cont in patt as set, working in st st throughout, until 80 rows in all have been worked from charts, ending with a ws row.
### Shape armholes
Keeping patt correct, cast off 6 sts at beg of next 2 rows and 2 sts at beg of foll 4 rows. 138 sts.**
Now work straight (working in A only when chart is complete) until back measures 23cm (9in) from beg of armhole shaping, ending with a ws row.
### Shape shoulders
Cast off 17 sts at beg of next 4 rows, and 15 sts at beg of

CHART 2

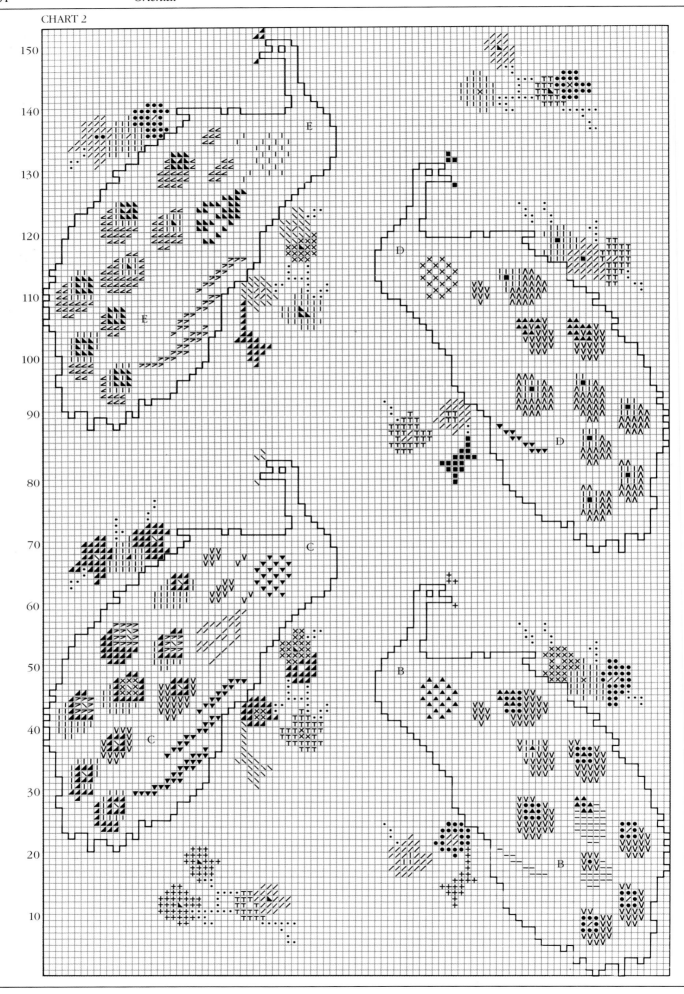

CHART 1      rep 1st – 40th rows

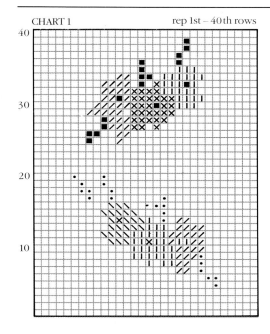

CHART 3      rep 1st – 40th rows

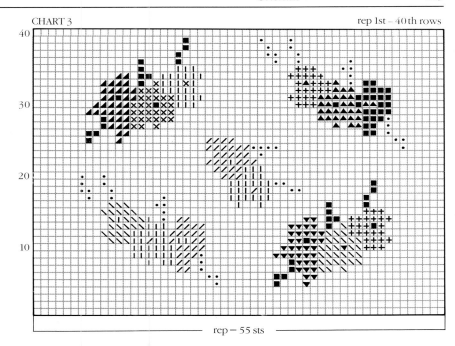

rep = 55 sts

foll 2 rows.
Cast off rem 40 sts.

## FRONT
Work as given for back to **
Now work straight (working in A only when chart is complete) until front measures 19.5cm (7¾in) from beg of armhole shaping, ending with a ws row.

### Divide for neck
**Next row** Patt 53 sts, turn, leaving rem sts on a spare needle, and cont on these sts only for first side of neck.
Dec 1 st on every row until 49 sts rem.
Now work straight until front matches back to beg of shoulder shaping, ending at armhole edge.

### Shape shoulder
Cast off 17 sts at beg of next and foll alt row. 15 sts.
Work 1 row.
Cast off.
With rs of work facing, return to sts on spare needle, rejoin yarn to next st, cast off centre 32 sts, patt to end. 53 sts.
Complete second side of neck to match first side, reversing shapings.

## SLEEVES
Using 3mm (US2) needles and yarn A, cast on 62 sts.
Work 2cm (¾in) in K1, P1 rib.
Change to 3¼mm (US3) needles and work in cable rib as given for back until sleeve measures 15cm (6in) from cast-on edge, ending with a ws row.
**Next row** K7, (inc in next st) to last 7 sts, K7. 110 sts.
**Next row** P to end.
Now commence colour patt from chart 3, working in st st throughout, *at the same time* inc 1 st at each end of next and every foll 4th row until there are 140 sts on needle.
Work straight until sleeve measures 48cm (19in) from cast-on edge, ending with a ws row.

### Shape top
Cast off 6 sts at beg of next 2 rows, and 2 sts at beg of next 4 rows, then dec 1 st at each end of every row until 92 sts rem.
Cast off.

## TO MAKE UP
Join right shoulder and neckband seam.
### Neckband
With rs of work facing, using 3mm (US2) needles and

□ = A unless otherwise indicated
⊞ = B    ⅃⅃ = N
◨ = C    ⊡ = Q
◼ = D    ⊠ = R
◨ = E    ▲ = S
▼ = F    ▼ = T
◉ = G    ⊓ = U
◩ = H    ◥ = V
◩ = J    ◲ = W
⊟ = L
◪ = M

*Bright blues and grapy pinks offer a complete contrast to the muted Peacock on page 103.*

yarn A, K up 102 sts evenly around neck edge.
Work 7 rows in K1, P1 rib.
Cast off in rib.
Join left shoulder seam to 5cm (2in) from neckband, so leaving final cast-off section open.
### Crochet neck edging
Using 2.50mm (USC) crochet hook and yarn D, work picot edging as foll:
**1st row** Work in double crochet around neck edge and shoulder seam opening.
**2nd row** *1 double crochet into each of next 3 double crochet, 4 chain, slipstitch into last double crochet; rep from * around neck edge only.
Work 3 button loops spaced evenly along neckband and shoulder seam opening.
Sew on buttons opposite button loops.
Set in sleeves.
Join side and sleeve seams.

# *Apple Branch*

Taken from a detail of garlands surrounding a Venetian painting. I enjoyed the clusters of flowers on a dark ground which gave a rather oriental feel. The design works just as well with a plain rib in place of the lattice.

■ = A

CHART 1                                    rep from 1st row

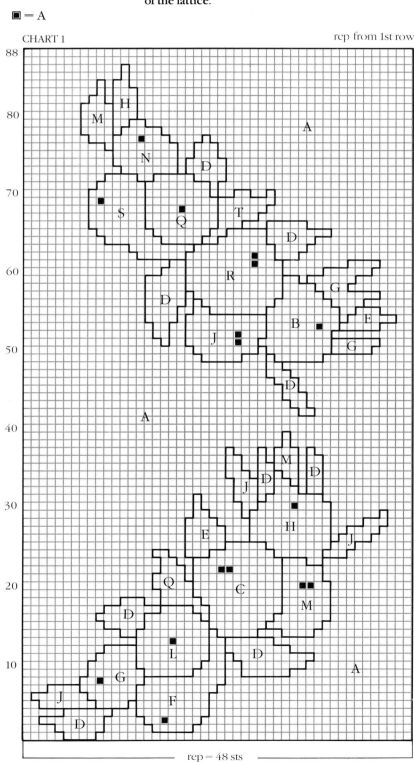

rep = 48 sts

## SIZE

**Adult's sweater**
**To fit** one size only up to 91cm (36in) bust
**Actual width measurement** 104cm (41in)
**Length to shoulder** 65.5cm (25¾in)
**Sleeve seam** 51cm (20in)
**Child's cardigan**
**To fit** one size only up to 71cm (30in) chest
**Actual width measurement** 89cm (35in)
**Length to shoulder** 35cm (13¾in)
**Sleeve seam** 48cm (19in) cuff unfolded

## MATERIALS

**Adult's sweater**
400g (15oz) four-ply wool in main colour (A)
50g (2oz) in first contrast colour (B)
25g (1oz) in each of 14 contrast colours
(C,D,E,F,G,H,J,L,M,N,Q,R,S,T)
**Child's cardigan**
200g (8oz) four-ply wool in main colour (A)
25g (1oz) in each of 13 contrast colours
(B,C,D,E,F,G,H,J,L,M,N,Q,R)
1 pair each 2¾mm (US1) and 3¼mm (US3) needles
2 buttons (adult's)
9 buttons (child's)

## TENSION

28 sts and 36 rows to 10cm (4in) over patt on 3¼mm (US3) needles.

## SPECIAL ABBREVIATIONS

*Tw2l(AB)* – twist 2 left with yarns A and B as foll: miss 1st st on left-hand needle and K tbl 2nd st with yarn A, then K 1st st with yarn B, slipping both sts off needle at the same time.
*Tw2l(BA)* – twist 2 left with yarns B and A as foll: miss 1st st on left-hand needle and K tbl 2nd st with yarn B, then K 1st st with yarn A, slipping both sts off needle at the same time.
*Tw2r(AB)* – twist 2 right with yarns A and B as foll: miss 1st st on left-hand needle and K 2nd st with yarn A, then K 1st st with yarn B, slipping both sts off needle at the same time.
*Tw2r(BA)* – twist 2 right with yarns B and A as foll: miss 1st st on left-hand needle and K 2nd st with yarn B, then K 1st st with yarn A, slipping both sts off needle at the same time.

## ADULT'S SWEATER

### BACK

Using 2¾mm (US1) needles and yarn A, cast on 146 sts.
Work 2cm (¾in) in K1, P1 rib.
Change to 3¼mm (US3) needles and work in lattice patt as foll (carry yarn very loosely across ws of work to avoid puckering):
**1st row** (ws) P to end.
**2nd row** K1A, *Tw2l(AB), K4A, Tw2r(BA); rep from * to last st, K1A.
**3rd and every alt row** P all the A sts in A, and all the B sts in B.
**4th row** K2A, *Tw2l(AB), K2A, Tw2r(BA), K2A; rep from * to end.

**6th row** K3A, *Tw2l(AB), Tw2r(BA), K4A; rep from *, ending last rep K3A.
**8th row** K4A, *Tw2r (using B for both sts), K6A; rep from *, ending last rep K4A.
**10th row** K3A, *Tw2r(BA), Tw2l(AB), K4A; rep from *, ending last rep K3A.
**12th row** K2A, *Tw2r(BA), K2A, Tw2l(AB), K2A; rep from * to end.
**14th row** K1A, *Tw2r(BA), K4A, Tw2l(AB); rep from * to last st, K1A.
**16th row** K1A, 1B, 6A, *Tw2l (using yarn B for both sts), K6A; rep from * to last 2 sts, K1B, 1A.
**17th row** As 3rd row.
The 2nd–17th rows form lattice patt rep.
Cont in lattice patt until back measures 12cm (4¾in) from cast-on edge, ending with a ws row.
Now beg apple branch patt from chart 1, working in st st throughout, using separate lengths of yarn for each colour area and twisting yarns tog at colour joins to avoid holes, as foll:
**1st row** (rs) K1A, (patt 1st row of chart 1) 3 times, K1A.
This row sets position of chart patt.
Cont in apple branch patt until 100 rows have been

*Apple Branch in soft dove grey (right) and cream chenille (below).*

worked from chart 1, ending with a ws row.
**Shape armholes**
Keeping patt correct, cast off 5 sts at beg of next 2 rows, then 3 sts at beg of foll 2 rows. 130 sts.
Now work straight until 129 rows in all have been worked from chart, thus ending with 41st chart row.
**Next row** P10A, (work 42nd row of chart 1) twice, P to end in A.
This row sets position of chart patt.**
Cont in patt until 25.5cm (10in) have been worked from beg of armhole shaping. Cast off.

## FRONT
Work as given for back to **.
Cont in patt until work measures 12 rows less than back to shoulder, ending with a ws row.
**Divide for neck**
**Next row** Patt 45 sts, turn, leaving rem sts on a spare needle and cont on these sts only for first side of neck.
Dec 1 st at neck edge on every row until 34 sts rem.
Now work straight until front matches back to cast-off row. Cast off.
With rs of work facing, return to sts on spare needle, rejoin yarn to next st, cast off 40 sts, patt to end. 45 sts.
Complete second side of neck to match first, reversing shapings.

## RIGHT SLEEVE
Using 2¾mm (US1) needles and yarn A, cast on 58 sts.
Work 5cm (2in) in K1, P1 rib.
Change to 3¼mm (US3) needles and work 34 rows in lattice patt as given for back, *at the same time* inc 1 st at each end of every foll 3rd row, working the incs into patt. 80 sts.
Now beg apple branch patt from chart as foll:
**1st row** (rs) K16A, patt 1st row of chart, K16A.
This row sets position of chart.
Cont in patt, *at the same time* inc on every 3rd row as before until there are 150 sts.
Now work straight until sleeve measures 51cm (20in) from cast-on edge (when 88 rows of chart are completed, cont in A only).
**Shape top**
Cast off 5 sts at beg of next 2 rows, then 3 sts at beg of foll 2 rows. Cast off rem 134 sts.

## LEFT SLEEVE
Work as given for right sleeve, but work 41st–88th rows of chart 1 first, then 1st–40th rows, to reverse motifs.

## COLLAR
Using 3¼mm (US3) needles and yarn A, cast on 154 sts.
Work 15cm (6in) in lattice patt as for back.
Cast off.

## TO MAKE UP
Join shoulder seams.
Join cast-on edge of collar to neck edge, beg at left shoulder seam, so that back edge ends 1cm (½in) in from left shoulder seam.
Fold collar in half on to ws and catch down.
**Front collar edging**
Using 3mm (US2) needles and yarn A, K up 24 sts along front collar opening through both edges of fold.
Work 2 rows in K1, P1 rib.
**1st buttonhole row** Rib 4, cast off 2 sts, rib 12 including st used to cast off, cast off 2 sts, rib to end.
**2nd buttonhole row** Rib to end casting on 2 sts over those cast off in previous row.
Rib 2 rows. Cast off in rib.
**Back collar edging**
Work as for front collar edging, omitting buttonholes.
Join side and sleeve seams.
Set in sleeves. Sew on buttons.

# CHILD'S CARDIGAN

## RIGHT FRONT

Using 3mm (US2) needles and yarn A, cast on 5 sts.
Work in K1 tbl, P1 rib, beg with a ws row, *at the same time* cast on 5 sts at beg of next and every foll alt row until there are 60 sts.
Rib 6 rows straight, ending with a ws row.
Change to 3¼mm (US2) needles and work 2 rows in st st, beg with a K row.
Now work in colour patt from chart 2, working in st st throughout and using separate lengths of yarn for each colour area, twisting yarns tog at colour joins to avoid holes as foll:
**1st row** (rs) Patt 1st row of chart between right front markers, K8A.
**2nd row** P8A, patt 2nd row of chart between right front markers.
These 2 rows set the position of patt.
Cont as set, work 55 rows, ending with a rs row.
**Shape armhole**
Cast off 6 sts at beg of next row. 54 sts.
Work 2 rows straight.
**Shape neck**
Dec 1 st at neck edge on next and foll 7 alt rows. 46 sts.
(Work 2 rows straight, then dec 1 st at neck edge on 3 foll alt rows) twice. 40 sts.
Now dec 1 st at neck edge on every foll 3rd row until 34 sts rem.
Now work straight until front measures 17cm (6¾in) from beg of armhole shaping, ending at armhole edge. (When chart is complete, cont in A only.)
**Shape shoulder**
Cast off 12 sts at beg of next row, and 11 sts at beg of foll alt row.
Work 1 row. Cast off.

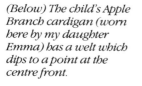

*(Below) The child's Apple Branch cardigan (worn here by my daughter Emma) has a welt which dips to a point at the centre front.*

## LEFT FRONT

Work as given for right front, reversing rib shaping and placing chart patt as foll:
**1st row** (rs) K8A, patt 1st row of chart between left front markers.
**2nd row** Patt 2nd row of chart between left front markers, P8A.
Cont as set and complete as for right front, reversing all shapings, working 1 row less before armhole shaping.

## BACK

Using 3mm (US2) needles and yarn A, cast on 124 sts.
Work 6 rows in K1 tbl, P1 rib.
Change to 3¼mm (US3) needles and work in colour patt from chart as foll:
**1st row** (rs) K14A, patt 1st row of chart, K14A.
**2nd row** P14A, patt 2nd row of chart, P14A.
These 2 rows set position of chart patt.
Cont as set, work 54 rows more, ending with a ws row.
**Shape armholes**
Cast off 6 sts at beg of next 2 rows. 112 sts.
Work straight until back matches fronts to shoulder, ending with a ws row.
**Shape shoulders**
Cast off 12 sts at beg of next 2 rows and 11 sts at beg of foll 4 rows.
Cast off rem 44 sts.

## RIGHT SLEEVE

Using 3mm (US2) needles and yarn A, cast on 40 sts.
Work 10cm (4in) in K1 tbl, P1 rib.
Change to 3¼mm (US3) needles and work 16 rows in st st, *at the same time* inc 1 st at each end of 11th and foll 4th row. 44 sts.
Now work in colour patt from chart between right

CHART 2

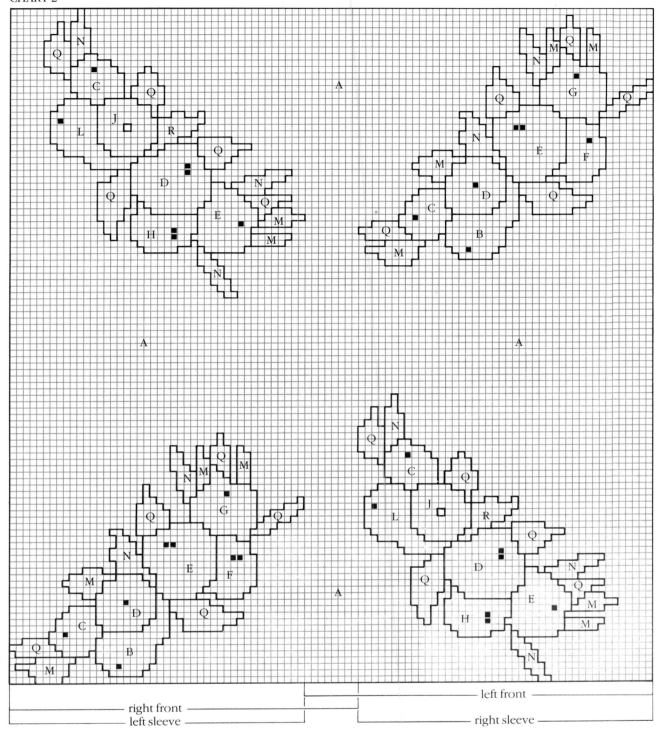

right front —————
left sleeve —————
————— left front —————
————— right sleeve —————

sleeve markers, rep 1st–64th rows only, and cont to inc on every 4th row from previous inc (working incs in A) until there are 94 sts.
Cast off.

**LEFT SLEEVE**
Work as given for right sleeve but between left sleeve markers and rep 1st–60th rows only.

**TO MAKE UP**
Join shoulder seams.
**Front band**
Using 3mm (US2) needles and yarn A, cast on 7 sts. Work in K1 tbl, P1 rib until band when slightly stretched fits up left front to beg of neck shaping, sewing band in position as you go.

Mark position of 9 buttons, one at beg of neck shaping, one 1cm (½in) from cast-on edge, and the rest spaced evenly between.
Cont to work in rib until band fits around neck edge and down right front, making buttonholes opposite button markers as foll:
**1st row** (rs) Rib 2, cast off 3 sts, rib to end.
**2nd row** Rib to end, casting on 3 sts over those cast off in previous row.
Cast off in rib.
Sew on front band.
Set in sleeves flat, matching centre of cast-off edge to shoulder seam and sewing last few rows of sleeve to cast-off sts at underarm.
Join side and sleeve seams.
Sew on buttons.

■ = A

# Ellipses

I love these flying saucer elliptical shapes, and simply enjoyed varying the size and colour of them. They are used here on a boxy double-breasted jacket with a mosaic shawl collar that concentrates the colours used in the ellipses.

## SIZE
**To fit** one size only up to 101cm (40in) bust
**Actual width measurement** 117cm (46in)
**Length to shoulder** 65cm (25½in)
**Sleeve seam** 47cm (18½in)

## MATERIALS
575g (22oz) Rowan Double Knitting Wool in black 62 (A)
100g (4oz) each in rowan 45 (B) and dark olive 606 (C)
50g (2oz) each in birch olive 59 (D), deep aubergine 99 (E), copper 18 (F), deep ochre 9 (G), emerald 124 (H), brick 412 (J), loden 89 (L), puce 601 (M) and buddleia 127 (N)
**Equivalent yarn** double knitting
1 pair each 3mm (US2) and 3¼mm (US3) needles
3mm (US2) and 3¼mm (US3) circular needles
14 buttons

*NOTE: A yarn kit is available for this design. See page 143 for details.*

## TENSION
27 sts and 36 rows to 10cm (4in) over patt on 3¼mm (US3) needles.

## BACK
Using 3mm (US2) needles and yarn A, cast on 158 sts.
Work 4cm (1½in) in K1, P1 rib.
Change to 3¼mm (US3) needles and work in colour patt from chart 1, working in st st throughout, until back measures 43cm (17in) from cast-on edge, ending with a ws row.
**Shape raglan armholes**
**Dec 1 st at each end of next 3 rows.
Work 1 row.**
Rep from ** to ** 19 times more. 38 sts. Cast off.

## RIGHT FRONT
Using 3mm (US2) needles and yarn A, cast on 96 sts.
Work 2cm (¾in) in K1, P1 rib, ending with a ws row.
**1st buttonhole row** (rs) Rib 34, cast off 3 sts, rib to end.
**2nd buttonhole row** Rib to end, casting on 3 sts over those cast off in previous row.
Now cont in rib until 4cm (1½in) have been worked from cast-on edge, ending with a ws row.
Change to 3¼mm (US3) needles and work in colour patt from chart 1, working between right front markers, work 18 rows.
Now rep 1st and 2nd buttonhole rows, working in chart patt rather than rib.
Rep last 20 rows 5 times more.
Now cont in patt until right front measures same as back to beg of armhole shaping, ending with a ws row.

**Shape raglan armhole**
***Dec 1 st at armhole edge on next 3 rows. Work 1 row.***
Now rep from \*\*\* to \*\*\* 19 times more, *at the same time* dec 1 st at front opening edge on next and 34 foll alt rows. Fasten off.

**LEFT FRONT**
Work as given for right front, omitting buttonholes and reversing all shapings.

**SLEEVES**
Using 3mm (US2) needles and yarn A, cast on 52 sts.

Work 10cm (4in) in K1, P1 rib.
**Next row** (ws) P into front and back of each st. 104 sts.
Change to 3¼mm (US3) needles and work in patt from chart 1, beg at 7th row, *at the same time* inc 1 st at each end of every foll 3rd row until there are 140 sts. Keeping patt correct, work straight until sleeve measures approx 47cm (18½in) from cast-on edge and patt matches back and fronts to beg of armhole shaping, ending with a ws row.
**Shape top**
Work as given for back from \*\* to \*\* 10 times. 80 sts. Dec 1 st at each end of every row until 2 sts rem. Fasten off.

☐ = A    ◩ = G
◪ = B    ■ = H
◉ = C    ◨ = J
◩ = D    ⊟ = L
◧ = E    ⊡ = M
◉ = F    ⊤ = N

CHART 1

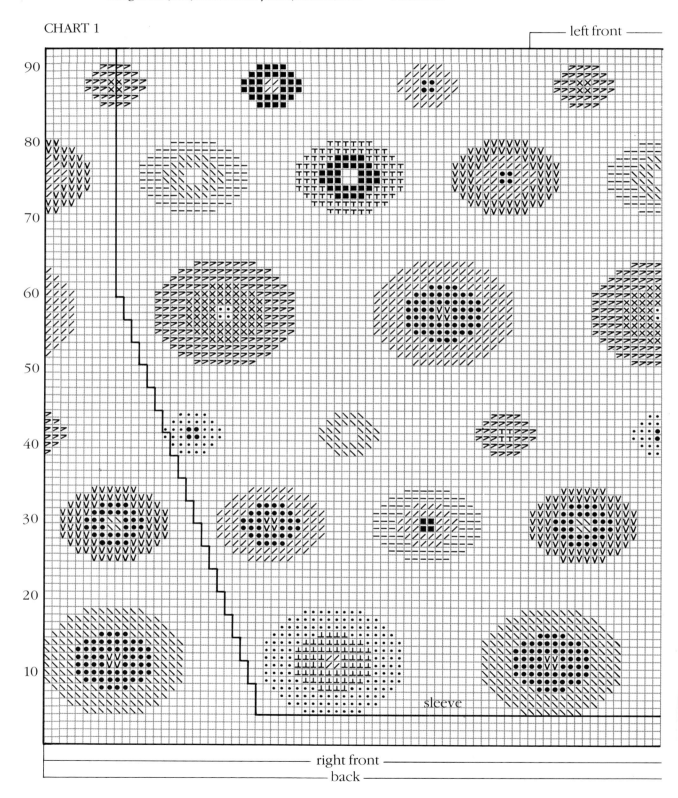

left front

right front

back

sleeve

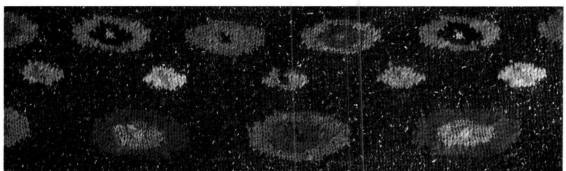

*The Ellipses colours echo the flecks in the blue/green tweed.*

rep from 1st row

— left front —

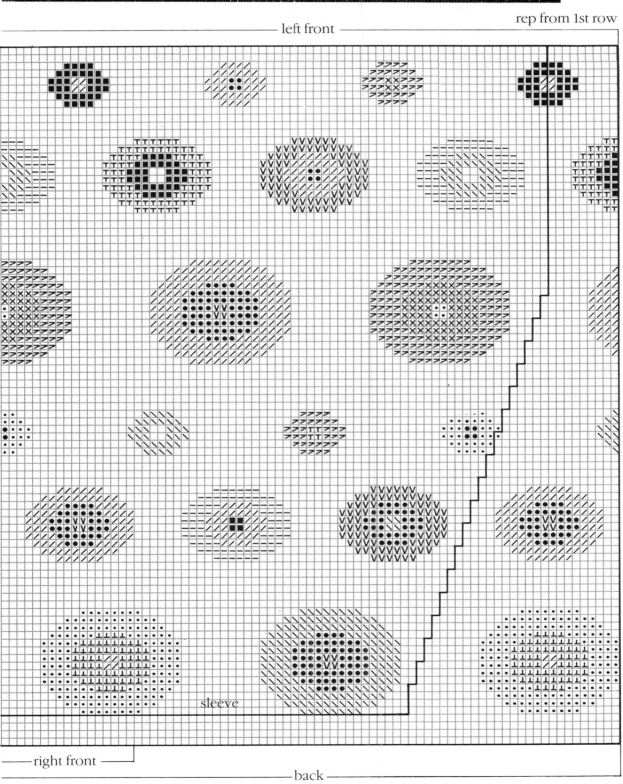

sleeve

— right front —

— back —

## RIGHT FRONT BAND

Using 3mm (US2) needles and yarn A, cast on 11 sts.
Work in rib as foll:
**1st row** (rs) K1 tbl, (P1, K1 tbl) to end.
**2nd row** P1, (K1 tbl, P1) to end.
Rep these 2 rows until band, when slightly stretched,
fits up right front opening edge to 6 rows below beg
of neck shaping, *at the same time* make buttonholes
opposite those on right front as foll:
**1st buttonhole row** (rs) Rib 4, cast off 3 sts, rib to end.
**2nd buttonhole row** Rib to end, casting on 3 sts over
those cast off in previous row.
Work 3 tog at outer edge of next 5 rows.
Fasten off.

## LEFT FRONT BAND

Work as for right front band omitting buttonholes, and
reversing shaping.

## COLLAR

Using 3¼mm (US3) needles and yarn A, cast on 2 sts.
Work in st st, inc 1 st at each end of 2nd and every foll
row until there are 38 sts, *at the same time* work
left-hand half of collar in colour patt from chart 2
(cont to work right-hand half in A only), ending with
20th row of chart.
Now work straight as foll:
**Next row** K19A, patt 21st row of chart.
**Next row** Patt 22nd row of chart, P15A, K4A.
**Next row** K19A, patt 23rd row of chart.
**Next row** Patt 24th row of chart, P15A, K4A.

Cont in this way, rep 19th–72nd chart rows until
unshaped part of collar measures 61cm (24in), ending
with a rs row.
Now, keeping patt correct, but working in st st only,
dec 1 st at each end of every row until 2 sts rem.
Fasten off.

## COLLAR EDGING

Beg at cast-on edge of collar, with rs facing, using
3¼mm (US3) circular needle and yarn B, K up 212 sts
evenly along join between main colour and chart patt,
ending at cast-off edge. Work in rows.
Work 6 rows in st st, beg with a P row.
Now pick up first st in B in K-up row and P it tog with
first st on left-hand needle, then P tog second st in
K-up row with second st on left-hand needle, and so
on across the row (make sure that the sts are correctly
lined up so that the piping remains smooth and
untwisted).
Change to 3mm (US2) circular needle and yarn A.
K 1 row.
Work 5 rows in K1, P1 rib. Cast off in rib.

## TO MAKE UP

Join raglan seams, side and sleeve seams.
Sew on front bands.
Fold collar in half along the edging, place edge of
ribbing in line with outer edge of front band, and join
on to neck edge, easing to fit, with the patterned half
falling to the outside.
Sew on buttons.

*(Previous page) The same double-breasted jacket shape worked in chenilles and, on the pink colourway, with diamonds replacing the ellipses, this is easily adapted from the basic pattern.*

*(Opposite) Ellipses in another mood.*

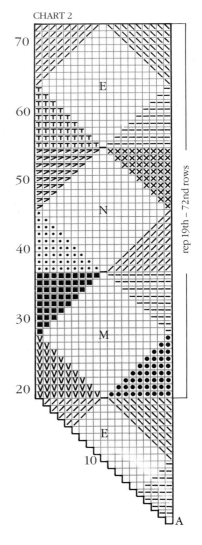

CHART 2

□ = A
☑ = B
⊡ = C
◩ = D
☒ = E
⊡ = F
☑ = G
■ = H
◨ = J
⊟ = L
⊤ = N

rep 19th – 72nd rows

# COUNTRY

# *Ducks*

With a name like Duckworth, I felt the book *had* to include a ducks design – and I do have a collection of those lovely old wooden decoy ducks. I worked the moss-stitch chevron pattern behind the ducks to suggest a shimmering watery backdrop.

## SIZE
**Adult's sweater**
**To fit** one size only up to 96cm (38in) bust/chest
**Actual width measurement** 104cm (41in)
**Length to shoulder** 73.5cm (29in)
**Sleeve seam** 54.5cm (21½in)
**Child's sweater**
**To fit** one size up to 71cm (30in) chest
**Actual width measurement** 78cm (30¾in)
**Length to shoulder** 54.5cm (21½in)
**Sleeve seam** 44cm (17¼in)

## MATERIALS
**Adult's sweater**
600g (22oz) Rowan Light Tweed in autumn 205 (A)
50g (2oz) Fine Fleck Tweed in rose 410 (B)
25g (1oz) each in emerald 124 (J), gold 14 (L) and
    purple 99 (R)
50g (2oz) Rowan Lightweight Double Knitting each in
    dark brown 80 (C), denim 615 (D), puce 602 (E),
    deep lilac 93 (F), ginger 403 (G), soft pink 109 (H),
    black 62 (M), loden 89 (N), red rust 77 (Q) and
    candy 95 (S)
**Equivalent yarn** four-ply
**Child's sweater**
400g (8oz) four-ply wool in main colour (A)
25g (1oz) each in 14 contrast colours
    (B,C,D,E,F,G,H,J,L,M,N,Q,R,S)
1 pair each 3mm (US2) and 3¼mm (US3) needles

*NOTE: A yarn kit is available for this design. See page 143 for details.*

## TENSION
31½ sts and 37 rows to 10cm (4in) over chart patt on 3¼mm (US3) needles.

## SPECIAL ABBREVIATIONS
*Tw2r* (twist 2 right) – miss 1st st on left-hand needle and K 2nd st, then K 1st st, slipping both sts off needle at the same time
*Tw2l* (twist 2 left) – miss 1st st on left-hand needle and K tbl 2nd st, then K 1st st, slipping both sts off needle at the same time
*ytf* – yarn to front

## ADULT'S SWEATER

*Strangely, although the ducks are the same size on the adult as well as the child's version (worn here by my son Oliver), the scale seems right in both.*

### BACK
Using 3mm (US2) needles and yarn A, cast on 134 sts.
Work 2.5cm (1in) in K1, P1 rib.
**Next row** Rib 8, *inc in next st, rib 3, rep from * to last 10 sts, inc in next st, rib 9. 164 sts.
Change to 3¼mm (US3) needles and work in chevron patt as foll (sl all sts P-wise):

**1st row** (ws) P to end.
**2nd row** K1, *Tw2r, K8; rep from * to last 3 sts, Tw2r, K1.
**3rd row** P1, *sl 2, P8; rep from * to last 3 sts, sl 2, P1.
**4th row** K2, *Tw2l, K6, Tw2r; rep from * to last 2 sts, K2.
**5th row** K1, P1, * K1, ytf, sl 1, P6, sl 1, P1; rep from * to last 2 sts, K1, P1.
**6th row** P1, K1, *P1, Tw2l, K4, Tw2r, K1; rep from * to last 2 sts, P1, K1.
**7th row** (K1, P1) twice, *sl 1, P4, sl 1, (K1, P1) twice; rep from * to end.
**8th row** (P1, K1) twice, *Tw2l, K2, Tw2r, (P1, K1) twice; rep from * to end.
**9th row** K1, *(P1, K1) twice, ytf, sl 1, P2, sl 1, P1, K1; rep from * to last 3 sts, P1, K1, P1.
**10th row** P1, *(K1, P1) twice, Tw2l, Tw2r, K1, P1; rep from * to last 3 sts, K1, P1, K1.
**11th row** *(K1, P1) 3 times, sl 2, K1, P1; rep from * to last 4 sts, (K1, P1) twice.
**12th row** *(P1, K1) 3 times, Tw2r, P1, K1; rep from * to last 4 sts, (P1, K1) twice.
**13th row** (K1, P1) to end.
**14th row** P1, *Tw2r, (K1, P1) 4 times; rep from * to last 3 sts, Tw2r, K1.
**15th row** K1, *ytf, sl 2, (P1, K1) 4 times; rep from * to last 3 sts, ytf, sl 2, K1.
**16th row** K2, *Tw2l, (P1, K1) 3 times, Tw2r; rep from * to last 2 sts, K2.
**17th row** P3, *sl 1, (K1, P1) 3 times, sl 1, P2; rep from * to last st, P1.
**18th row** K3, *Tw2l, (K1, P1) twice, Tw2r, K2; rep from * to last st, K1.
**19th row** P4, *sl 1, (P1, K1) twice, ytf, sl 1, P4; rep from * to end.
**20th row** K4, *Tw2l, P1, K1, Tw2r, K4; rep from *.
**21st row** P5, *sl 1, K1, P1, sl 1, P6; rep from *, ending last rep P5.
**22nd row** K5, *Tw2l, Tw2r, K6; rep from *, ending last rep K5.
**23rd row** P6, *sl 2, P8; rep from *, ending last rep P6.
**24th row** K6, *Tw2r, K8; rep from *, ending last rep K6.
These 24 rows form chevron patt.
Now work in colour patt from chart 1, using separate lengths of yarn for each colour area and twisting yarns tog at colour joins to avoid holes, as foll:
**1st row** (ws) P20, patt 1st row of chart, P21.
**2nd row** K21, patt 2nd row of chart, K20.
These 2 rows set position of chart patt.
Cont in patt, working ducks in st st throughout and background in st st and chevron patt as shown on chart, until 168 rows in all have been worked from chart.
**Shape armholes**
Keeping chart patt correct, cast off 8 sts at beg of next 2 rows. 148 sts. Now work 82 rows straight**.
Now cont in chevron patt, work 48 rows, then cont in st st until work measures 26cm (10¼in) from beg of armhole, ending with a P row.
**Shape shoulders**
Cont in st st, cast off 8 sts at beg of next 8 rows and 5 sts at beg of foll 2 rows.
Cast off rem 74 sts.

**FRONT**
Work as given for back to **.
Cont in chevron patt, work 22 rows.
**Divide for neck**
Keep chevron patt correct for a further 26 rows, then
cont in st st.
**Next row** (ws) Patt 59 sts, turn, leaving rem sts on a
spare needle and cont on these sts for first side of neck.
Cont in chevron patt, dec 1 st at neck edge on every
row until 37 sts rem.
Now work straight until front matches back to
shoulder, ending at armhole edge.
**Shape shoulder**
Cast off 8 sts at beg of next and foll 3 alt rows.
Work 1 row. Cast off rem 5 sts. With ws of work facing,
return to sts on spare needle, rejoin yarn to next st,
cast off 30 sts, patt to end. Complete second side of
neck to match first, reversing shapings.

**SLEEVES**
Using 3mm (US2) needles and yarn A, cast on 54 sts.
Work 8cm (3in) in K1, P1 rib.
**Next row** *Rib 1, inc 1; rep from * to end of row. 84
sts.
Change to 3¼mm (US3) needles and work 4 rows in
st st, beg with a P row.
Now work 120 rows in chevron patt, *at the same time*
inc 1 st at each end of every foll 3rd row, ending with a
24th patt row. 164 sts.
Now work in colour patt from chart as foll:
**Next row** P41, work 1st row of chart between sleeve
markers, P41.
**Next row** K41, work 2nd row of chart between sleeve
markers, K41.
These 2 rows set the position of chart patt.
Cont as set, work 82 rows more.
Cast off.

□ = A    ● = J
☒ = B    · = L
◩ = C    ◪ = M
· = D    △ = N
☑ = E    ⊞ = Q
☑ = F    Ⅱ = R
⊟ = G    ◤ = S
◩ = H

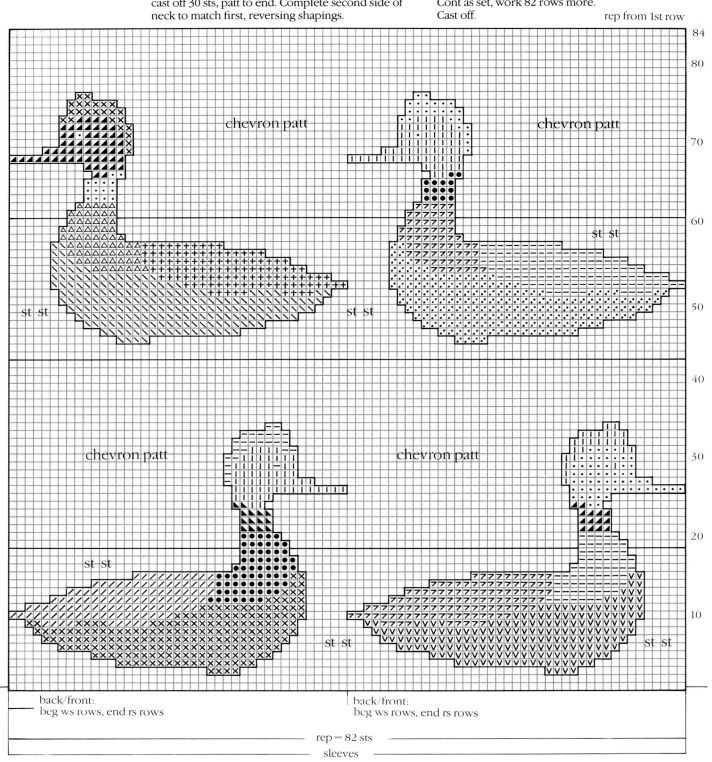

rep from 1st row

chevron patt          chevron patt

st st          st st

chevron patt          chevron patt

st st          st st

back/front:
beg ws rows, end rs rows

back/front:
beg ws rows, end rs rows

—— rep = 82 sts ——

—— sleeves ——

## TO MAKE UP
Join right shoulder seam.

**Neckband**

With rs of work facing, using 3mm (US2) needles and yarn A, K up 22 sts down left side of front neck, 30 sts across front neck, 22 sts up right side of front neck and 58 sts across back neck. 132 sts.

Work 9 rows in K2, P2 rib. Cast off in rib.

Join left shoulder and neckband seam.

Set in sleeves, matching centre of cast-off edge to shoulder seam and joining last few rows of sleeve to cast-off sts at underarm.

Join side and sleeve seams.

# CHILD'S SWEATER

## BACK

Using 3mm (US2) needles and yarn A, cast on 124 sts.

Work 7.5cm (3in) in K1 tbl, P1 rib.

Work 24 rows in chevron patt as given for adult sweater, ending with a rs row.

Work 2 rows in st st, beg with a P row.

Now work in colour patt from chart, as foll:

**1st row** (ws) P21A, patt 43rd row of chart, P21A.

**2nd row** K21A, patt 44th row of chart, K21A.

These 2 rows set chart position.

Cont as set, working ducks in st st throughout, and background in chevron patt and st st as shown on chart work 45th–84th chart rows, then 1st–84th rows, ending with a rs row.**

Now work 34 rows in chevron patt.

Cast off, marking centre 54 sts for back neck.

## FRONT

Work as given for back to **.

Now work 24 rows in chevron patt.

**Divide for neck**

**Next row** Patt 40 sts, turn, leaving rem sts on a spare needle and cont on these sts for first side of neck.

Dec 1 st at neck edge on next and 4 foll alt rows.

Cast off rem 35 sts.

With ws of work facing return to sts on spare needle, rejoin yarn to next st, cast off 44 sts, patt to end. 40 sts.

Complete second side of neck to match first reversing shapings.

## SLEEVES

Using 3mm (US2) needles and yarn A, cast on 50 sts.

Work 7.5cm (3in) in K1 tbl, P1 rib.

**Next row** Inc 1, rib 2, inc 1, (rib 3, inc 1) to last 2 sts, rib 1, inc 1. 64 sts.

Work 3 rows in st st, beg with a K row.

Now work 60 rows in chevron patt, *at the same time* inc 1 st at each end of every foll 3rd row. 104 sts.

Now work in chart patt as foll:

**1st row** (ws) P11A, patt 1st row of chart, P11A.

**2nd row** K11A, patt 2nd row of chart, K11A.

These 2 rows set chart position.

Cont as set, inc on next and every foll 5th row until there are 122 sts.

Then work straight until 84 rows have been worked from chart. Work 4 rows in st st, beg with a P row.

Cast off.

## TO MAKE UP
Join right shoulder seam.

**Neckband**

Using 3mm (US2) needles and yarn A, K up 10 sts down left front neck, 42 sts across front neck, 10 sts up right front neck and 52 sts across back neck. 114 sts.

Work 7 rows in K1 tbl, P1 rib. Cast off in rib.

Join left shoulder and neckband seams.

Set in sleeves flat, matching centre of cast-off edge to shoulder seam. Join side and sleeve seams.

# Silver Birch

This is remotely based on a painting by Gustav Klimt – silver birch trees on a carpet of autumn leaves. Although it now bears no resemblance to the source, that was my jumping-off point.

## SIZE

To fit one size only up to 111cm (44in) bust/chest
**Actual width measurement** 149cm (58¾in)
**Length to shoulder** 70cm (27½in)
**Sleeve seam** 54cm (21¼in)

## MATERIALS

400g (15oz) four-ply yarn in main colour (A)
50g (2oz) in each of 13 contrast colours (B,C,D,E,F,G,H,J,N,Q,R,S,T)
25g (1oz) in each of two contrast colours (L,M)
1 pair each 3mm (US2) and 3¼mm (US3) needles

## TENSION

24 sts and 36 rows to 10cm (4in) over chart patt on 3¼mm (US3) needles.

## SPECIAL INSTRUCTIONS

**Cable 1**
Worked over 18 sts in yarn A.
**1st row** (rs) P1, K1, (P2, K2) 3 times, P2, K1, P1.
**2nd and every alt row** K1, P1, K2, (P2, K2) 3 times, P1, K1.
**3rd and 5th rows** As 1st row.
**7th row** P1, K1, P2, K2, P2, sl next 4 sts on to cable needle and hold at back of work, K2, then sl 2 P sts from cable needle back on to left-hand needle and P them, then K2 from cable needle, P2, K1, P1.
**9th and 11th rows** As 1st row.
**13th row** P1, K1, P2, sl next 4 sts on to cable needle and hold at front of work, K2, then sl 2 P sts from cable needle back on to left-hand needle and P them, then K2 from cable needle, P2, K2, P2, K1, P1.
The 2nd–13th rows form the patt rep.
**Cable 2**
Worked over 12 sts in yarn A.
**1st row** (rs) P3, K6, P3.
**2nd and every alt row** K3, P6, K3.
**3rd row** As 1st row.
**5th row** P3, sl next 3 sts on to cable needle and hold at back of work, K3, then K3 from cable needle, P3.
**6th row** As 2nd row.
The 1st–6th rows form the patt rep.

## BACK

Using 3mm (US2) needles and yarn A, cast on 204 sts.
Work 5cm (2in) in K2, P2 rib.
Change to 3¼mm (US3) needles and work in cable and colour patt, using separate lengths of yarn for each colour area, twisting yarns tog at colour joins to avoid holes, and working chart in st st throughout, as foll:
**1st row** (rs) (Patt 1st row of chart 1, 1st row of cable 1, 1st row of chart 2, 1st row of cable 2) twice, 1st row of chart 1, 1st row of cable 1.
**2nd row** (Patt 2nd row of cable 1, 2nd row of chart 1,

2nd row of cable 2, 2nd row of chart 2) twice, 2nd row of cable 1, 2nd row of chart 1.
These 2 rows set position of cable and colour patt.
Cont as set until back measures 43cm (17in) from cast-on edge, ending with a ws row.
**Shape armholes**
Cast off 3 sts at beg of next row and 5 sts at beg of foll row, (cast off 3 sts at beg of next row and 4 sts at beg of foll row) 4 times. 168 sts.**
Now work straight until back measures 27cm (10½in) from beg of armhole shaping.
Cast off, marking 55th st for end of right shoulder.

## FRONT

Work as given for back to **
Now work straight until front measures 22cm (8½in) from beg of armhole shaping, ending with a ws row.
**Divide for neck**
**Next row** Patt 69 sts, turn, leaving rem sts on a spare needle and cont on these sts only for first side of neck.
Dec 1 st at neck edge on every row until 54 sts rem.
Work straight until front matches back to cast-off edge.
Cast off.
With rs of work facing return to sts on spare needle, cast off 35 sts, patt to end. 64 sts.
Complete second side of neck to match first side, reversing shaping, and dec to 52 sts instead of 54.

*(Overleaf) Silver Birch and Ellipses (page 112) at the piano.*

work in st st throughout

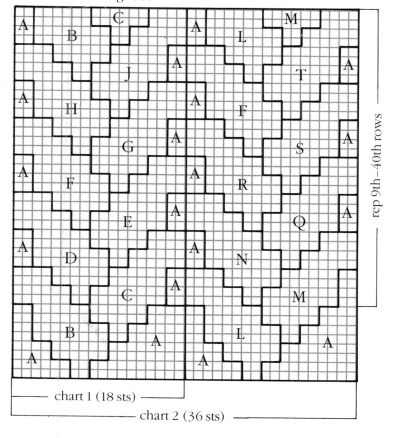

chart 1 (18 sts)
chart 2 (36 sts)
rep 9th–40th rows

## SLEEVES
Worked from sleeve top to cuff.
Using 3¼mm (US3) needles and yarn A, cast 126 sts.
Work in cable and colour patt as foll:
**1st row** (rs) Beg with 7th st, patt rem 30 sts of 1st row of chart 2, 1st row of cable 2, 1st row of chart 1, 1st row of cable 1, 1st row of chart 2, 1st row of cable 2.
This row sets position of cable and colour patt.
### Shape top
Cast on 4 sts at beg of next row and 6 sts at beg of foll row, then (cast on 5 sts at beg of next row and 3 sts at beg of foll row) 4 times, working extra sts into rem chart 2 and cable 1 at right edge, and chart 1 at left edge. 168 sts.
Cont as set at *the same time* dec 1 st at each end of every foll 5th row until 108 sts rem.
Now work straight until sleeve measures 47cm (18½in) from cast-on edge, ending with a ws row.

Change to 3mm (US2) needles and yarn A.
**Next row** K4, (K2 tog) to last 4 sts, K4. 54 sts.
Work 10cm (4in) in K2, P2 rib.
Cast off in rib.

## TO MAKE UP
Join right shoulder seam.
### Neckband
With rs of work facing using 3mm (US2) needles and yarn A, K up 16 sts down left side of front neck, 34 sts across front neck, 16 sts up right front neck and 60 sts across back neck. 128 sts.
Work 9 rows in K2, P2 rib.
Cast off in rib.
Join left shoulder and neckband seam.
Set in sleeve, matching centre of cast-on edge to shoulder seam.
Join side and sleeve seams.

*A sage green version of the Silver Birch sweater.*

# *Oak Leaves*

A tapestry cushion from Hardwick Hall in Derbyshire gave me the idea for this cardigan design. The arrangement of these lovely oak-leaf shapes was what drew me to it, and they proved a marvellously versatile vehicle for different colourways.

## SIZES
**To fit** 91[96]cm (36[38]in) bust
**Actual width measurements** 100[111]cm (39½[43¾]in)
**Length to shoulder** 66.5cm (26¼in)
**Sleeve seam** 47[50]cm (18½[19¾]in)

## MATERIALS
300[350]g (11[13]oz) four-ply yarn in main colour (A)
25g (1oz) in each of 10 contrast colours (B,C,D,E,F,G,H,J,L,M)
1 pair each 3mm (US2) and 3¼mm (US3) needles
3mm (US2) circular needle
Cable needle
9 buttons

## TENSION
28 sts and 36 rows to 10cm (4in) over chart patt on 3¼mm (US3) needles.

## SPECIAL ABBREVIATION
*cable 4* – sl next 2 sts on to cable needle and hold at front of work, K2, then K2 from cable needle

## BACK
Using 3mm (US2) needles and yarn A, cast on 138[152] sts.
Work 10 rows in K1, P1 rib.
Change to 3¼mm (US3) needles and work in cable patt and colour patt from chart 1, using separate lengths of yarn for each colour area, twisting yarns tog at colour joins to avoid holes, as foll:
**1st row** (rs) K4[11], P2, K4, P2, K20, P2, K4, P2, K4, patt 1st row of chart 1, K4, P2, K4, P2, K20, P2, K4, P2, K4[11].
**2nd row** P4[11], K2, P4, K2, P20, K2, P4, K2, P4, patt 2nd row of chart, P4, K2, P4, K2, P20, K2, P4, K2, P4[11].
**3rd, 5th and 7th rows** As 1st row but working 3rd, 5th and 7th rows of chart.
**4th, 6th and 8th rows** As 2nd row but working 4th, 6th and 8th rows of chart.
**9th row** K4[11], P2, cable 4, P2, K20, P2, cable 4, P2, K4, patt 9th row of chart, K4, P2, cable 4, P2, K20, P2, cable 4, P2, K4[11].
**10th row** As 2nd row but working 10th row of chart.
These 10 rows form patt rep for cable patt at each side of chart and set position of chart patt.
Rep 1st–10th rows for cables, and work 11th–86th rows of chart, then 1st–60th rows, ending with a ws row.
### Shape armholes
Cast off 12 sts at beg of next 2 rows. 114[128] sts.
Now work straight until 1st–86th chart rows have been worked twice, then work 1st–56th rows.
Work 2 more rows completing existing motifs only.
Cast off.

## LEFT FRONT
Using 3mm (US2) needles and yarn A, cast on 68[76] sts. Work 10 rows in K1, P1 rib.
Change to 3¼mm (US3) needles and work in cable and chart patts as foll:
**1st row** (rs) K4[12], P2, K4, P2, K4, patt 1st row of chart, K2.
**2nd row** P2, patt 2nd row of chart, P4, K2, P4, K2, P4[12].
These 2 rows set position of chart and cable patt as given for back.
Cont as set until left front matches back to armhole, ending with a ws row.
### Shape armhole
Cast off 12 sts at beg of next row. 56[64] sts.
Now work 18 rows straight.
### Shape neck
Keeping patt correct, dec 1 st at neck edge on next and rep from 1st row

*(Overleaf) Autumn leaves! The Oak Leaves and Silver Birch sweaters in vibrant russet tones.*

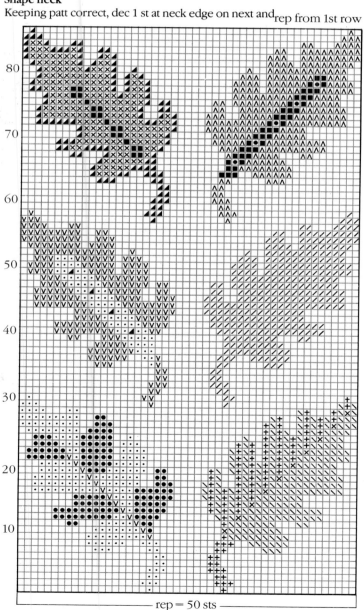

rep = 50 sts

□ = A
☑ = B
◪ = C
⊡ = D
☑ = E
☒ = F
⊞ = G
◉ = H
◪ = J
■ = L
△ = M
□

every foll 3rd row, until 36[42] sts rem.
Work straight until left front matches back to cast-off edge.
Cast off.

## RIGHT FRONT

Work as given for left front, reversing placing of cable patt and all shapings, by working 1 more row before armhole shaping and 1 row less before neck shaping.

## SLEEVES

Using 3mm (US2) needles and yarn A, cast on 55 sts.
Work 10cm (4in) in K1, P1 rib.
**Next row** Rib 5, (K into front and back of next st, rib 9) to end. 60 sts.
**Next row** (Rib 1, K into front and back of next st) to end. 90 sts.
Change to 3¼mm (US3) needles and work in cable and chart patt as foll:
**1st row** (rs) K8, P2, K4, P2, K4, patt 1st row of chart, K4, P2, K4, P2, K8.
This rows sets position of chart and cable patt as given for back.
Cont as set, *at the same time* inc 1 st at each end of next and every foll 5th row until there are 130 sts, working extra sts into st st.
Now work straight until 1st–86th rows, then 1st–56th rows have been worked from chart.
Work 2 more rows to complete existing motifs only, then cont in st st in A until sleeve measures 53[56]cm (21[22]in) from cast-on edge. Cast off.

## TO MAKE UP

Join shoulder seams.
**Armbands**
With rs of work facing, using 3mm (US2) circular needle and yarn A, K up 12 sts from cast-off at underarm, 114 sts around armhole and 12 sts across cast-off. 138 sts. Work in rows.
**Next row** (P1, K1 tbl) 6 times, work 2 tog, work in K1 tbl, P1 rib to last 14 sts, work 2 tog, rib to end.
**Next row** Rib to end.
Rep last 2 rows twice more. Cast off in rib.
**Collar and front bands**
Using 3mm (US2) needles and yarn A, cast on 11 sts.
Work in K1 tbl, P1 rib until band when slightly stretched fits up left front edge to beg of neck shaping, sewing band in position as you go.
Mark the position of 9 buttons on this band, one at beg of neck shaping, one 2cm (¾in) from cast-on edge and the rest spaced evenly between.
Now cont in rib, *at the same time* inc 1 st at outer edge on every row until there are 28 sts.
Now work straight until collar fits to centre back neck.
Cast off in rib.
Now work second half of collar and front band reversing shaping, and making buttonholes on band opposite button markers as foll:
**1st buttonhole row** Rib 4, cast off 3 sts, rib to end.
**2nd buttonhole row** Rib to end, casting on 3 sts over those cast off in previous row.
Finish sewing on collar and front bands.
**Collar edging**
Beg at left front collar edge, using 3mm (US2) circular needle and yarn A, K up 200 sts around collar edge.
Work in rows.
Work 4 rows in K1 tbl, P1 rib, dec 1 st at each end of every row. 192 sts. Cast off in rib.
Set in sleeves inside armbands.
Join side and sleeve seams, leaving armbands free.
Sew on buttons.

*The Oak Leaves chart can be adapted to many shapes. Here I've used it on the Ellipses jacket (far left) and on a crew-neck sweater (left).*

# Gloves

## SIZE
**To fit** an average hand
**Actual width across palm** approx 10cm (4in)

## MATERIALS
Approx 50g (2oz) four-ply yarn in chosen colours
1 pair each 3mm (US2) and 3¼mm (US3) needles

## TENSION
28 sts and 36 rows to 10cm (4in) over st st on 3¼mm (US3) needles.

## RIGHT-HAND GLOVE
Using 3mm (US2) needles, cast on 56 sts.
Work 7.5cm (3in) in K2, P2 rib.
Change to 3¼mm (US3) needles and work in st st as foll:
**Shape thumb gusset**
**1st row** (rs) K28, inc into next st, K1, inc into next st, K25.
**2nd–6th rows** Work in st st, beg with a P row.
**7th row** K28, inc into next st, K3, inc into next st, K25.
**8th–10th rows** Work in st st, beg with a P row.
**11th row** K28, inc into next st, K5, inc into next st, K25.
**12th–14th rows** Work in st st, beg with a P row.
**15th row** K28, inc into next st, K7, inc into next st, K25.
**16th–18th rows** Work in st st, beg with a P row.
**19th row** K28, inc into next st, K9, inc into next st, K25.
**20th–22nd rows** Work in st st, beg with a P row.
**23rd row** K28, inc into next st, K11, inc into next st, K25. 68 sts.
Work 11 rows straight.**
**Next row** K44, turn and cast on 2 sts.
**Next row** P18, turn and cast on 2 sts.
***Work on these 20 sts for thumb, work 20 rows in st st, ending with a P row.
**Shape top**
**Next row** (K2 tog, K2) 5 times. 15 sts.
**Next row** P to end.
**Next row** (K2 tog) 7 times, K1. 8 sts.
Break off yarn and thread through rem sts. Fasten off.
Sew up thumb seam.
With right-hand needle, K up 4 sts from base of thumb, K to end. 56 sts.
Now work 15 rows in st st, ending with a P row.
**Shape first finger**
**Next row** K36, turn and cast on 1 st.
**Next row** P17, turn and cast on 1 st.
Work on these 18 sts for first finger, work 22 rows in st st, ending with a P row.
**Next row** (K2 tog, K2) 4 times, K2. 14 sts.
**Next row** P to end.
**Next row** (K2 tog) 7 times. 7 sts.
Break off yarn and thread through rem sts. Fasten off.
Sew up finger seam.
**Shape second finger**
With right-hand needle K up 2 sts from base of first finger, K7, turn and cast on 1 st.
**Next row** P17, turn and cast on 1 st.
Work on these 18 sts for second finger, work 26 rows. Complete as given for first finger.

**Shape third finger**
Work as given for second finger but work 22 rows instead of 26. Complete as given for first finger.
**Shape fourth finger**
With right-hand needle, K up 2 sts at base of third finger, K6. 14 sts.
Now work 20 rows in st st, ending with a P row.
**Next row** (K2, K2 tog) 3 times, K2. 11 sts.

*Among this collection of gloves, I have used motifs and sections of several of the charted designs in the book including Fruits, Moths, Wild Roses, Pansies and Oak Leaves. The pattern is given for*

*the basic glove shape, allowing you to add whatever design you please.*

**Next row** P to end.
**Next row** (K2 tog) 5 times, K1. 6 sts.
Complete as for first finger. Sew up side seam.

**LEFT-HAND GLOVE**
Work to match right glove, reversing position of thumb gusset as foll:

**1st row** (rs) K25, inc into next st, K1, inc into next st, K28.
**2nd–6th rows** A right glove.
**7th row** K25, inc into next st, K3, inc into next st, K28.
Cont reversing thumb gusset in this manner to **
**Next row** K40, turn and cast on 2 sts.
**Next row** P18, turn and cast on 2 sts.
Cont as given for right glove from *** to end.

# Reading the Patterns

The patterns in this book are written in a fairly
standard form so they will, I hope, be perfectly
comprehensible to all averagely competent knitters.
Nevertheless there are a few points which may be
worth emphasizing for less experienced knitters, or
for those whose skills are, perhaps, a little rusty.

## SIZES

Many of the patterns provide instructions for several
sizes. The smallest size is given first with the larger
sizes following in square brackets. When choosing
which size to knit, look at the *actual* measurements as
well as the *to fit* measurement. Many of the garments
are generously sized and you may wish to choose a
size which will give you a tighter fit (or, indeed, *vice
versa*). The sizes are given in metric with non-metric
equivalents in the following parentheses. When
following measurements through a pattern, use
metric *or* non-metric measurements consistently.
Don't jump from one to the other.

## MATERIALS

In the patterns for which there are kits (see page 143),
the yarns and colours used to complete the design are
specified. Elsewhere only generic yarns are quoted
and in these cases you can use any suitable four-ply or
double knitting or whatever *providing* it can be
knitted up to the correct tension (this means that, to
be on the safe side, you should make a tension check
with one ball before buying enough yarn for the
whole garment). Where generic yarns are quoted the
quantities can only be approximate; much depends on
the precise composition of the yarn used. We have
tried to be generous with the yarn allocations, but if
you don't mind having yarn left over, then buy a few
extra balls.

Many of the designs use lots of different colours,
some only in very small quantities. So since 25g (1oz)
and sometimes 50g (2oz) are the smallest quantities
you can buy, it can happen that there is lots of yarn left
over. Many knitters welcome this as it replenishes
their yarn store and provides lots of choice for
experiments and future projects. But if you wish to be
as economical as possible, and a kit is being offered,
that is often the most efficient way to buy the yarns as
they are wound off in much more accurate quantities.

## CHARTS

Many of the designs in this book are worked from
charts which are drawn with symbols rather than
colours. If you find it difficult to follow the design
through the chart, it can be helpful to photocopy that
page of the book and hand-colour it. Many copying
machines will also enlarge the charts if you find the
squares too small.

*(Left) These are working swatches for some of my
many experiments with interlace basketweave
patterns.*

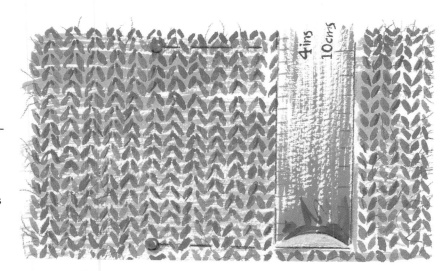

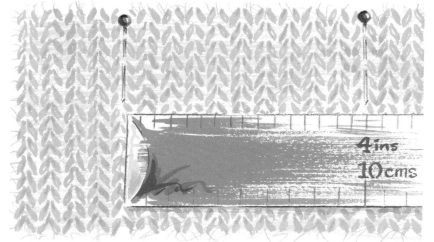

## TENSION

It is essential to check your tension before beginning
to knit up a design. If your tension is not accurate your
sweater or cardigan will not be the right size and the
yarn quantities may be inadequate. Remember that
the needle size given is only a recommendation.
Some knitters may have to adjust the size up or down
to achieve the tension given in the pattern.

To check your tension knit up a sample using the
yarn specified in the Materials section and the stitch
and needle size specified in the Tension section. (If it
is a colour pattern, make sure you handle the yarn
exactly as specified; this can make all the difference to
the tension.) Then count the number of stitches and
rows in your sample. If there are more stitches or
rows to 10cm (4in) than there should be, your sample
is too tight and you should knit up another one on
larger needles. If there are fewer stitches or rows to
10cm (4in) than there should be, your sample is too
loose and you should knit up another one using
smaller needles. Keep on adjusting the needle size
until the correct tension is obtained.

*To measure row tension
(top): place a ruler or
tape measure alongside
one column of stitches as
shown. Insert a pin at the
zero and 10cm (4in)
marks. Count the stiches
between the pins.*

*To measure stitch tension
(above): place a ruler or
tape measure under one
row of stitches. Insert a
pin at the zero and 10cm
(4in) marks. Count the
stitches between the pins.*

## HANDLING YARNS

There are several methods which may be used to handle lots of different coloured yarns in multi-coloured patterns. They vary depending on the nature of the colour pattern – whether it is an all-over repeating pattern like Fair Isle, for example, or several separate motifs on a plain ground, and on whether the areas of colour are small or large, covering one or two stitches, or many. Fortunately you do not have to decide for yourself which method to use. The pattern will specify it precisely and it is very important to use the method specified or the tension of the garment will be altered. The two commonest methods are Fair Isle and intarsia.

## FAIR ISLE METHOD

The Fair Isle method is appropriate where only two or three colours are used in a row, and where the spans between the colours are short. The yarns not in use are either stranded (or 'floated') across the back of the work, or woven into each other in the course of making the stitches. When stranding yarn, it is particularly important to carry it very loosely across the back. If it is pulled too tightly the fabric will be puckered.

## INTARSIA METHOD

The intarsia method is the one used in most of the patterns in this book. It is appropriate when many different colours are being used in a row, or when lots of separate motifs are being worked. By this method the yarns are twisted together at each colour join and then left in position to be worked on the next row.

When many different yarns are being used it can be difficult to avoid them becoming dreadfully tangled at the back of the work. If you use fairly generous lengths of yarn instead of balls, at least they can easily be pulled free of the tangle.

*The Fair Isle method: (top) stranding in a knit row; (above) stranding in a purl row; (right) weaving yarns into the back of the work.*

*The intarsia method.*

## SWISS DARNING

Swiss darning is an embroidery stitch which exactly mimics the structure of knitted stocking stitch. It is a useful technique where small spots of colour are needed in a design. Instead of working them in with the rest of the knitting, Swiss-darn them on afterwards. Swiss darning can also be used to correct mistakes or to effect changes of mind about colours after the design is completed. But it does tend to thicken the fabric so it's only really successful over small areas.

To work Swiss darning (right) use a yarn that is the same weight as the background fabric so that the stitches are evenly covered. Insert the needle through the base of the first stitch (*a*), then behind the base of the stitch above from *b* to *c*. Then take the needle back through the base of the first stitch (*d*) and out through the base of the second stitch to be covered (*e*).

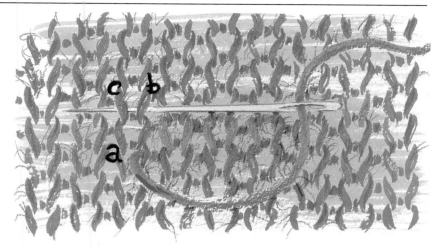

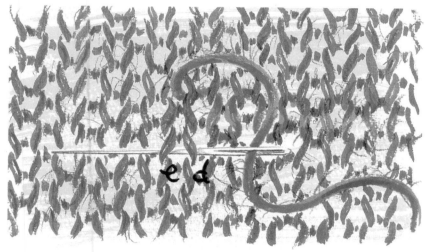

## FINISHING

When many colours are used in a design, the darning in of loose ends after the knitting is finished can be dauntingly laborious. If you knit them in as you go by wrapping the ends around the main colour thread for two or three stitches beyond where they were last used, the job will be much easier.

All garments should be blocked before being sewn up. Use a thick towel or blanket as a soft pad and pin out each piece of the garment to the correct measurements. If the fabric is textured (cabled or ribbed, for example) it should be lightly sprayed with water and left to dry naturally. But Fair Isle or other flat coloured patterns often benefit from a good press with a damp cloth.

Sew up using backstitch seams for joins which run parallel with rows (like shoulder seams). Invisible seams are ideal for joining two pieces of stocking stitch where the join runs at right angles to the rows (like side seams, for example).

*(Left) Invisible seaming.*

# Abbreviations

| | | |
|---|---|---|
| alt – alternately | K – knit | rs – right side of work |
| approx – approximately | K up – pick up and knit | sl – slip |
| beg – begin(ning) | mm – millimetres | st(s) – stitches |
| cm – centimetre(s) | P – purl | st st – stocking stitch (stockinette stitch) |
| cont – continu(e)(ing) | patt – pattern | tbl – through back of loop(s) |
| dec – decreas(e)(ing) | psso – pass slipped stitch over | tog – together |
| foll – follow(s)(ing) | p2sso – pass 2 slipped stitches over | ws – wrong side of work |
| g – grams | rem – remain(s)(ing) | yo – yarn over |
| in – inch(es) | rep – repeat(s) | wyif – with yarn in front of work |

# Hints for American Knitters

American knitters will have few problems in working from English patterns and *vice versa*. The following tables and glossaries should prove useful.

## TERMINOLOGY

| UK | US |
|----|----|
| cast off | bind off |
| catch down | tack down |
| double crochet | single crochet |
| stocking stitch | stockinette stitch |
| Swiss darning | duplicate stitch |
| tension | gauge |

All other terms are the same in both countries.

## YARN EQUIVALENTS
The following table shows the approximate yarn equivalents in terms of thickness. However, it is always essential to check the tension of substitute yarns before buying enough for the whole garment.

| UK | US |
|----|----|
| four-ply | sport |
| double knitting | knitting worsted |
| Aran-weight | fisherman |
| chunky | bulky |

## METRIC CONVERSION TABLES

### Length
(to the nearest ¼in)

### Weight
(rounded up to the nearest ¼oz)

| cm | in | cm | in | g | oz |
|----|----|----|----|----|----|
| 1 | ½ | 55 | 21¾ | 25 | 1 |
| 2 | ¾ | 60 | 23½ | 50 | 2 |
| 3 | 1¼ | 65 | 25½ | 100 | 3¾ |
| 4 | 1½ | 70 | 27½ | 150 | 5½ |
| 5 | 2 | 75 | 29½ | 200 | 7¼ |
| 6 | 2½ | 80 | 31½ | 250 | 9 |
| 7 | 2¾ | 85 | 33½ | 300 | 10¾ |
| 8 | 3 | 90 | 35½ | 350 | 12½ |
| 9 | 3½ | 95 | 37½ | 400 | 14¼ |
| 10 | 4 | 100 | 39½ | 450 | 16 |
| 11 | 4¼ | 110 | 43½ | 500 | 17¾ |
| 12 | 4¾ | 120 | 47 | 550 | 19½ |
| 13 | 5 | 130 | 51¼ | 600 | 21¼ |
| 14 | 5½ | 140 | 55 | 650 | 23 |
| 15 | 6 | 150 | 59 | 700 | 24¾ |
| 16 | 6¼ | 160 | 63 | 750 | 26½ |
| 17 | 6¾ | 170 | 67 | 800 | 28¼ |
| 18 | 7 | 180 | 70¾ | 850 | 30 |
| 19 | 7½ | 190 | 74¾ | 900 | 31¾ |
| 20 | 8 | 200 | 78¾ | 950 | 33¾ |
| 25 | 9¾ | 210 | 82¾ | 1000 | 35½ |
| 30 | 11¾ | 220 | 86½ | 1200 | 42¼ |
| 35 | 13¾ | 230 | 90½ | 1400 | 49¼ |
| 40 | 15¾ | 240 | 94½ | 1600 | 56½ |
| 45 | 17¾ | 250 | 98½ | 1800 | 63½ |
| 50 | 19¾ | 300 | 118 | 2000 | 70½ |

## NEEDLE SIZE CONVERSION TABLES
The needle sizes given in the patterns are recommended starting points for making tension samples. The needle size actually used should be that on which the stated tension is obtained.

| Metric | US | Old UK |
|--------|----|--------|
| 2mm | 0 | 14 |
| 2¼mm | 1 | 13 |
| 2½mm | | |
| 2¾mm | 2 | 12 |
| 3mm | | 11 |
| 3¼mm | 3 | 10 |
| 3½mm | 4 | |
| 3¾mm | 5 | 9 |
| 4mm | 6 | 8 |
| 4½mm | 7 | 7 |
| 5mm | 8 | 6 |
| 5½mm | 9 | 5 |
| 6mm | 10 | 4 |
| 6½mm | 10½ | 3 |
| 7mm | | 2 |
| 7½mm | | 1 |
| 8mm | 11 | 0 |
| 9mm | 13 | 00 |
| 10mm | 15 | 000 |

# Kits and Stockists

Some of the patterns in this book list the precise yarns and colours used in a particular design and colourway. These yarns are all Rowan Yarns and can be obtained at many of the usual yarn stockists as well as by mail order. Write to the addresses below for lists of stockists.

**United Kingdom**
Rowan Yarns
Green Lane Mill
Holmfirth
West Yorkshire
England HD7 1RW
*Tel. 0484 687714/5/6*

**USA**
Westminster Trading Corporation
5 Northern Blvd
Amherst
New Hampshire 03031
USA
*Tel. 603 886 5041*

**Canada**
Estelle Designs and Sales Ltd
38 Continental Place
Scarborough
Ontario
Canada M1R 2T4
*Tel. 416 298 9922*

**Australia**
Sunspun Enterprises Pty Ltd
195 Canterbury Road
Canterbury 3126
Victoria
Australia
*Tel. 3 830 1609*

**New Zealand**
Creative Fashion Centre
PO Box 45083
Epuni Railway
Lower Hutt
New Zealand
*Tel. 04 664 689*

**West Germany**
Textilwerkstatt
Friedenstrasse 5
3000 Hannover 1
West Germany
*Tel. 511 818001*

**Holland**
Henk & Henrietta Beukers
Dorpstraat 9
5327 AR Hurwenen
Holland
*Tel. 4182 1764*

**Denmark**
Mosekonens Vaerksted
Mosevej 13

L1 Binderup
9600 Aars
Denmark
*Tel. 8 656065*

**Norway**
Eureka
Kvakkestandgarden
1400 Ski
Norway
*Tel. 287 1909*

**Cyprus**
Colourworks
12 Parnithos Street
Nicosia
Cyprus
*Tel. 21 472933*

**Bermuda**
The Yarn Loft
PO Box DV 203
Devonshire DV BX
Bermuda
*Tel. 809 29 5 0551*

**Japan**
DiaKeito Co. Ltd
1-5-23 Nakatsu
Oyodo-Ku
Osaka 531
Japan
*Tel. 6 371 5653*

Yarn Kits are available for the following designs:
Wild Roses (jacket only, page 12)
Moths (page 16)
Pansies (page 19)
Blackwork (cardigan only, page 24)
Cable Grape (page 41)
Harlequin (page 52)
China Cardigan (oatmeal colourway, page 74)
Cabbage Rose (page 92)
Ellipses (black colourway, page 112)
Ducks (adult size only, page 122)

*Note: In some cases the yarn shade supplied may not match exactly the colour in the photograph.*

For information about kits write to the following addresses:

**UK and Europe**
Ehrman (mail order)
21/22 Vicarage Gate
London W8 4AA
England
*Tel. (01) 937 4568*

**USA**
Ehrman
5 Northern Blvd
Amherst
New Hampshire 03031
*Tel. 603 886 5054*

**Canada**
Estelle Designs and Sales Ltd
38 Continental Place
Scarborough
Ontario
Canada M1R 2T4
*Tel. 416 298 9922*

**Australia**
Sunspun Enterprises Pty Ltd
195 Canterbury Road
Canterbury 3126
Victoria
Australia
*Tel. 3 830 1609*

**New Zealand**
R. G. & P. A. Hoddinott
PO Box 1486
Auckland

# Acknowledgements

My special thanks to all the people who have helped me to complete this book. To Gail Rebuck, Sarah Wallace, Hugh Ehrman and Stephen Sheard for their constant encouragement, my editor Sandy Carr who very patiently helped me through, Marilyn Wilson for her technical expertise in translating my patterns, Kathleen Hargreaves for her help in sorting out the kits, Tony Boase for his lovely fashion shots, Gabi Tubbs for her clever styling, Keith Russell for his original design presentation and Christine Hanscomb for her beautiful still life photographs.

A big thank you to all those knitters and finishers who have spent so many painstaking hours knitting up my designs. To name but a few: Catherine Davies, Mary Kennard, Dianne Watson, Joyce Legg, Gail Berry, Shelia Saunders, Karen Naush, J. Dean, D. M. Hamlyn, Barbara Stokes, Bertha Fry, Joyce Robinson, B. Johns, M. Couch, E. Passell, A. M. Edworthy, Eileen Gooden, L. I. Allcock, J. Wood, J. Dalgleish, L. R. Lamb and M. R. Pearce. Thanks to Robin, Jane, Nan, Alan and Jenny for lending me various props.

Finally, thank you to my family and friends.

# Credits

Clothes were lent by Antiquarius–Julitta Y5 *pp 19, 21*; The Beauchamp Place Shop *pp 25, 49, 101*; Bymail *pp 67, 125*; Ally Capellino *pp 17, 49, 59, 69, 71, 75, 101, 123, 126, 128, 132, 133*; Nicole Farhi *p 13*; Dorin Frankfurt *p 53*; Valerie Goad *p 110*, Hobbs *p 103*; Jacadi *p 123*; Ralph Lauren *pp 39, 40, 61*; Liberty *pp 83, 84, 107*; Lunn Antiques *pp 67, 96, 97*; Marella *p 62*; Mulberry *pp 24, 29*; Sally Mee *pp 71, 119, 129*; Dries van Noten *pp 25, 28, 57*; Qui *pp 16, 17, 42*; Weekend *p 53*; Whistles *pp 31, 35, 39, 40, 43, 93, 113*. Hats by Antiquarius–Julitta Y5 *pp 19, 21, 57*; The Hat Shop *pp 31, 35, 39, 40, 53, 62, 113, 125*. Belts and bags by Mulberry *pp 13, 43, 57, 71, 103, 125*. Gloves by Antiquarius–Julitta Y5 *pp 25, 28, 75, 83, 84*; Dents *pp 13, 15, 45, 113*; Scarves by Antiquarius–Julitta Y5 *pp 24, 29, 117*; Liberty *p 13*; Lunn Antiques *p 61*; Scotch House *pp 15, 53*. Jewellery by Beaux Bijoux *p 107*; The Watch Gallery *p 57*. Glasses by Cutler & Gross *pp 25, 28*. Tights by Dior *pp 96, 97*.
Hair and make-up by Ruby Hammar, Katya Thomas and Llewellyn.
For the still life photography by Christine Hanscomb the oak chest was lent by Tony Bunzl and Zal Davar Antiques; dhurries by the General Trading Company; vases, bowls and rugs by Designers Guild; and dried flowers by Saville Edells, and Honeysuckle.

*The Harlequin cardigan, page 52.*